THE
NEW YORK
MAPGUIDE
Michael Middleditch

CONTENTS

PENGUIN BOOKS

THE NEW YORK SUBWAY SYSTEM

HOW TO USE THE SUBWAY MAP

The New York City subway system operates 24 hours a day, a 7-days-a-week service, but not all routes operate at all times. The basic service runs from **6am to midnight.**

59 Street
Columbus Circle
A·B·C·D·1·9

A **bold** letter or figure under or by a station name indicates that the route always operates, and trains stop at the station between 6am and midnight.

South Ferry
9

Terminus and line Number or Letter
Terminus et numéro ou lettre de ligne
Endstation mit Linien buchstaben oder nummern
Eindstation met Nummer of Letter de Linie
Terminali con Quotidiano Numeri o Cifre
Terminal con Número sea Letra de Linea

○ Delancey
Street

Interchange Station
Station de correspondance
Umsteigestation
Aansluiting op andere Lijnen
Station di coincidenza
Correspondencia

Chambers St.
M

Line Terminus and Interchange Station
Terminus et correspondance
Endstation mit Umsteigestation
Eindpunt met Aansluiting
Capolinea con coincidenza
Terminal con Correspondencia

━━ 9

Line and Colour
Ligne et couleur
Linie und Farbe
Lijnen met kleuren
Linea e colori
Línea y color

ROUTE	DESTINATIONS	NOTES
❶ ❾	242 Street/Bronx- South Ferry/Manhattan	*242 Street/Bronx terminal for Van Cortlandt Park.*
❷	241 Street/Bronx- Flatbush Av. Brooklyn	*East 180 St. for Bronx Zoo. Eastern Parkway for Brooklyn Museum. Grand Army Plaza for Prospect Park.*
❸	148 Street/Manhattan New Lots Av./Brooklyn	*Eastern Parkway for the Brooklyn Museum. Grand Army Plaza for Prospect Park.*
❹	Woodlawn/Bronx- Utica Avenue/Brooklyn	*161 Street/Bronx for the Yankee Stadium.*
❺ ❺	Nereid or Dyre Avs./Bronx- Flatbush Av./Brooklyn	*East 180 Street for the Bronx Zoo. Nereid Avenue/Bronx Rush Hours only.*
❻	Pelham Bay Park/Bronx- Brooklyn Bri./Manhattan	*Pelham Bay Park Terminal is approximately 2 miles from Orchard Beach and City Island.*
❼	Main St. Flushing/Queens- Times Square/Manhattan	*Willets Point/Queens for Shea Stadium - the National Tennis Center - Louis Armstrong Park and Stadium.*
Ⓐ Ⓐ Ⓐ Ⓐ HOWARD BEACH JFK	207 Street/Manhattan -Lefferts Blvd/Queens -Far Rockaway/Queens -Rockaway Park/Queens	*HOWARD BEACH for JFK AIRPORT - Take the Rockaway Park or Far Rockaway line for Manhattan. Direction 207 Street/Manhattan for the Cloisters Museum, get out at 190 Street Station.*
Ⓒ	*145 Street/Manhattan- Euclid Avenue/Brooklyn	**Rush hours - Bedford Park Boulevard, Bronx. Weekends 168 Street/Manhattan - World Trade Center*
Ⓖ	Smith-9 Streets/Brooklyn- 71-Continental Avs./Queens	*Evenings and weekends Queens Plaza/Queens Smith - 9 Streets/Brooklyn.*
Ⓙ Ⓩ	Broad Street/Manhattan- Jamaica Center/Queens	*The Z Service operates only during rush hours.*
Ⓑ Ⓑ Ⓑ	168 Street/Manhattan or 21 Street/Queens- Coney Island/Brooklyn	*Rush hours to 168 Street/Manhattan Evenings to 21 Street/Queens.*

ROUTE	DESTINATIONS		ROUTE	DESTINATIONS
Ⓔ	World Trade Center/Manhtn- Jamaica Center/Queens		Ⓛ	8 Avenue Manhattan- Rockaway Parkway/Brook.
Ⓓ	205 Street/Bronx- Coney Island/Brooklyn		Ⓝ	Ditmars Blvd/Queens- Coney Island/Brooklyn
Ⓕ	179 Street/Queens- Coney Island/Brooklyn		Ⓡ	71-Continental Avs./Queens -95 Street/Brooklyn
Ⓠ	21 Street/Queens- Brighton Beach/Brooklyn		Ⓜ	Metropolitan Av./Queens- Bay Parkway/Brooklyn
			Ⓢ	Shuttle Service Times Sq. to Grand Central

FOR TRAVEL INFORMATION
● (718) 330-1234 (06.00-21.00 Hrs.)

NON - ENGLISH SPEAKING
● (718) 330-4847 (07.00-19.00 Hrs.)

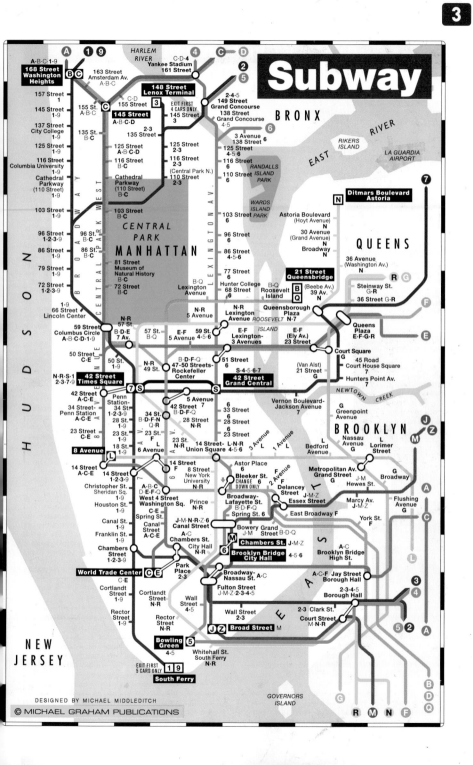

Subwauy

3

DESIGNED BY MICHAEL MIDDLEDITCH
© MICHAEL GRAHAM PUBLICATIONS

INTRODUCTION AND HISTORY

GEORGE AND THAT GRASSHOPPER

When I came to the decision to make another MAPGUIDE it was not hard to make New York my choice, for it gave me the chance to fulfill my early dreams in the city that epitomized for me at that time all that could be attained: like 'Hoppity' who had found a new life at the top of a skyscraper in my favorite cartoon, I too wanted to see this new life. In reality the lights were out in London and the aftermath of World War II had brought austerity to life in England. For this late traveller New York - Manhattan - in those days meant freedom, great noble skyscrapers (the tallest in the World) and music: the music I liked so much - the music that saw no reason to be the same every night. For me Manhattan was the real home of jazz; the melting pot that always metamorphosized itself, where new styles were developed (and still are). This is where I wanted to be. That glorious entrance with the Statue of Liberty off the shore welcoming you, George Gershwin's music, the tales of Damon Runyon, Broadway shows. Eddie Condon's, Birdland, the Manhattan skyline; these were the images that New York conjured for me.

FULFILLMENT

It was exciting: a frenetic, and restless, and yet stimulating place - the most diverse international city in the world. Everybody seems to be on stage. Inhibitions are shrugged off - often dangerously: rollerbladers, cyclists and even a legless guy propelling a wheelchair at over 30mph, beating the skaters - all of them vie for domination of the streets. People taking on traffic, a sight to behold. Brooklyn Bridge and the wondrous buildings of the early century still holding strong against their modern counterparts, making and augmenting the Manhattan magic, and Central Park, which surely must be the greatest urban park in the world. The contrasts: black guys often in trances with coffee cups begging - while uptown shops on Park Avenue drip with opulence: subway stations sorely needing attention - the superb buses that lower and tip to allow the aged and invalids on. Geysers of steam rising onto the sidewalks from the leaking pipes of the Edison Company's steam system which is still used for central heating. The constant craning upwards seeking the tops of buildings, often in early morning shrouded with clouds. Then there is Washington Square Park in the heart of Greenwich Village with the bookstalls on the sidewalks, New York University, jazz clubs and cafes all around, making the village something apart - something special.
Yes, I like New York.

KNICKERBOCKER GLORY

Always associated with commerce, New York was founded by the Dutch, although it was an Italian, Giovanni da Verrazano, who first sailed into New York harbor in 1524 - his name is given to the great bridge (1964) that connects Brooklyn with Staten Island. According to legend the Algonquian Indians bartered Manhattan Island for $24 worth of beads and ribbons. Peter Minuit, a Dutch West India Company employee, set up the deal; then the settlement was given the name New Amsterdam. By 1643 seventeen languages were being spoken, laying the foundations to eventually the world's most cosmopolitan city.

The last Dutch governor was the peg-legged Peter Stuyvesant who capitulated to the British under the Duke of York - later King James II. The town was then renamed New York, and Stuyvesant was allowed to retire to his farm or 'bowery'. Nine years later the settlement was retaken by the Dutch and returned by treaty one year later. Ten thousand people lived in the town by 1750, and it grew like no other place on earth. There were grammar schools, and King's College (now Columbia University), churches, synagogues and splendid houses.

BRAVE NEW WORLD

July 4th 1776 was a date destined to change the world: days later, on the common where City Hall now stands, George Washington paraded his volunteers and read the Declaration of Independence! That same day a gilded equestrian statue of George III was demolished; being made of lead it was melted down and made into bullets. A revolution was born, and the British were at war with their colony. When an attack was launched on Long Island - near Prospect Park - Brooklyn Heights was lost after a siege. Washington withdrew and was later defeated at Harlem (Morningside) Heights, forcing him to evacuate Manhattan Island: it remained under the control of the British until the end of the war in 1783, when he returned victoriously. Temporarily New York was the capital of the new republic but it was soon replaced by Philadelphia. The dollar became the currency, and eventually a stock exchange was established in 1817. Wall Street became the financial center as it is today.

ISLE OF JOY

Following the opening of the Erie Canal in 1825, the Great Lakes region became accessible: commerce, industry, railroads and steamships were developed, and immigration encouraged. New York became the largest city in America, the great seaport on the east-west commercial route. After the Civil War (1861-5), Black Americans began migrating from the South, and Chinese who had worked on the railroads arrived from the west coast: immigrants poured in from all over Europe, many getting turned back at Ellis Island. The lucky ones settled in ethnic neighborhoods, creating the diversity in the city's culture, and cheap labour! From Washington Square the expansion continued northwards, and although there were some of the worst slums in the world, there were examples to aspire to - people made it here! Mansions, hotels, theaters, concert halls and the magnificent Central Park were built. By 1902 the Flatiron building topped everything; from then on the city began reaching upwards for space. The colored neon lights on Broadway turned Manhattan into a pleasure island.

THE RESTLESS CITY

Perhaps it is this seeking of pleasure embodied in the joyous sculptured 'hares' of Barry Flanagan that adorn Park Avenue that really capture the spirit of the city. Manhattan is a vortex for all arts - they flourish and often are born here. It is surely no mistake that the United Nations chose New York as their base, where else could they go? There are monumental problems that need tackling in this town and no doubt time will produce more. New York is much too important, and its proven foundations are too strong to let the world pass it by. Liberty regenerates itself on $24 worth of real estate - Manhattan Island.

LOCATION MAP

SCALE

KILOMETRES

0   4   8

0   2   5

MILES

Oradell Reservoir

HASTINGS-ON-HUDSON

SPRAIN RIDGE COUNTY PARK

WESTCHESTER

YONKERS

PALISADES INTERSTATE PARK

TIBBETTS BROOK PARK

MOUNT VERNON

PATERSON

GARRET MOUNTAIN RESERVATION

N E W

HACKENSACK

ENGLEWOOD

OVERPECK COUNTY PARK

WAVE HILL

RIVERDALE PARK

VAN CORTLANDT PARK

GLENISLAND CASINO

J E R S E Y

GEORGE WASHINGTON BRIDGE

Spuyten Duyvil

THE CLOISTERS

BOTANICAL GARDENS

Poe Cottage

BRONX ZOO

PELHAM BAY PARK

ORCHARD BEACH

THE BRONX

CITY ISLAND

MONTCLAIR

(GIANTS STADIUM) MEADOWLANDS SPORTS COMPLEX

CROTONA PARK

Hackensack

NORTH BERGEN

MORRIS-JUMEL MANSION

YANKEE STADIUM

N E W

LONG ISLAND SOUND

THROGS NECK BRIDGE

Passaic

CENTRAL PARK

TRIBOROUGH BRIDGE

RIKERS ISLAND

EAST RIVER

BRONX-WHITESTONE BRIDGE

LA GUARDIA AIRPORT

KEARNY

WEEHAWKEN

MANHATTAN

STEINWAY

Y O R K

FLUSHING

MUSEUM OF THE MOVING IMAGE

SHEA STADIUM

HOBOKEN

LONG ISLAND CITY

Q U E E N S

EMPIRE STATE BUILDING

Newtown Creek

UNISPHERE (1964)

FLUSHING MEADOW CORONA PARK

NEWARK

LINCOLN PARK

JERSEY CITY

FOREST HILLS

BELMONT RACECOURSE

LIBERTY STATE PARK

STATEN ISLAND FERRY TERMINAL

WILLIAMSBURG

FOREST PARK

Ellis Island

L O N G

ST. ALBANS

NEWARK INTERNATIONAL AIRPORT

Governors Island

RED HOOK

PROSPECT PARK

I S L A N D

AQUEDUCT RACECOURSE

BAYONNE

Liberty Island

U P P E R B A Y

BROOKLYN

JOHN F. KENNEDY INTERNATIONAL AIRPORT

KILL VAN KULL

FERRY TERMINAL

FLATBUSH

GATEWAY

SILVER LAKE PARK

THE NARROWS

BAY RIDGE

SHORE ROAD PARK

NATIONAL RECREATION AREA

J A M A I C A B A Y

(NEW YORK)

S T A T E N

VERRAZANO-NARROWS BRIDGE

MARINE PARK

FLOYD BENNETT FIELD

I S L A N D

LA TOURETTE PARK

Hoffman Island

SHEEPSHEAD BAY

ROCKAWAY PARK

JACQUES MARCHAIS CENTER OF TIBETAN ART

Swinburne Island

CONEY ISLAND

NEW YORK AQUARIUM

BRIGHTON BEACH

ROCKAWAY INLET

JACOB RIIS PARK

RICHMOND

GATEWAY NATIONAL RECREATION AREA

Rockaway Point

S T A T E N I S L A N D

A T L A N T I C   O C E A N

A NEW YORK CALENDAR

JANUARY

WINTER ANTIQUES SHOW
Seventh Regiment Armory.   B5 23

NATIONAL BOAT SHOW
Jacob Javits Center.   **B2 34**

CHINESE NEW YEAR & DRAGON PARADE
Chinatown, Jan. 10th to early Feb.   **Page 43**

FEBRUARY

EMPIRE STATE BUILDING RUN-UP   **H3 35**

WESTMINSTER KENNEL CLUB DOG SHOW
Madison Square Garden.   **F3 35**

BLACK HISTORY MONTH
Events throughout the city.

NATIONAL ACADEMY OF DESIGN
Annual Exhibition.   **A5 24**

WASHINGTON'S BIRTHDAY PARADE
Fifth Avenue, February 22nd.   **Page 32**

MARCH

ST. PATRICK'S DAY PARADE
Fifth Avenue, March 17th.   **Page 32**

RINGLING BROTHERS and
BARNUM & BAILEY CIRCUS
Madison Square Garden.   **F3 35**

NEW YORK FLOWER SHOW
Passenger Ship Terminal, Pier 92.   **A4 30**

GOLDEN GLOVES FINALS
Madison Square Garden.   **F3 35**

APRIL

EASTER PARADE Fifth Av. on Easter Sunday.   32

INTERNATIONAL AUTOMOBILE SHOW
Madison Square Garden.   **F3 35**

ORCHID SHOW N.Y. Bot. Gdns. Bronx.   **Page 59**

BASEBALL SEASON commences.   **Page 54**

OPERA and BALLET Spring season.

MAY

FIVE BOROUGHS BIKE TOUR
Start and Finish at Battery Park.   **C5 46**

WASHINGTON SQ. Art Exhibition.   **G4 39**

CHERRY BLOSSOM FESTIVAL
Brooklyn Botanical Gardens.   **Page 60**

SoHo FESTIVAL   **Page 43**

MARTIN LUTHER KING Mem. Parade 5th Av.   32

JUNE

MUSEUM MILE
Fifth Avenue, 2nd Tues. Ten museums open free. 32

METROPOLITAN OPERA Free concerts in parks.

SUMMERPIER CONCERTS
South Street Seaport.   **F2 47**

PUERTO RICAN DAY PARADE Fifth Avenue.   32

GUGGENHEIM CONCERTS
Lincoln Center (D6 26) & Seaside Pk., Brooklyn.

BELMONT STAKES
Belmont Park Racecourse, Long Island.

SHAKESPEARE IN CENTRAL PARK
Free at the Delacorte Theater.   **F2 27**

GAY PRIDE MARCH. Last Sunday.

JULY

JVC JAZZ FESTIVAL
Venues in NYC in late June - early July.

INDEPENDENCE DAY
Celebrations and fireworks on the 4th July.

NEW YORK PHILHARMONIC Free in the parks.

AUGUST

GREENWICH VILLAGE JAZZ FESTIVAL   **P. 39**

LINCOLN CENTER OUTDOOR FESTIVAL **D6 26**

HARLEM WEEK
Fashion, Music, Art and Films. Mid August.

US OPEN TENNIS CHAMPIONSHIPS
Flushing Meadows, Queens.   **Page 54**

SEPTEMBER

CARNIVAL IN NEW YORK and
WIGSTOCK Labor Day.

WASHINGTON SQ. Art Exhibition.   **G4 39**

FESTIVAL OF SAN GENNARO
Mulberry Street, Little Italy.   **G2 43**

NEW YORK FILM FESTIVAL
Lincoln Center, late Sept - early Oct.   **D6 26**

FOOTBALL SEASON commences
Giants Stadium, New Jersey.   **Page 54**

MAYOR'S CUP SCHOONER RACE
South Street Seaport.   **F2 47**

NEW YORK PHILHARMONIC and
METROPOLITAN OPERA season commences.

OCTOBER

COLUMBUS DAY PARADE Fifth Avenue.   **P. 32**

HALLOWEEN PARADE Greenwich Village.   **P. 39**

HORSE RACING Aqueduct Racetrack, Queens.

ICE SKATING at Rockefeller Center.   **H4 31**

NOVEMBER

NEW YORK CITY MARATHON

VIRGINIA SLIMS Women's Tennis Champs., and

NATIONAL HORSE SHOW
Madison Square Garden.   **F3 35**

MACY'S THANKSGIVING DAY PARADE

DECEMBER

Christmas Spectacular at Radio City Music Hall,
and Christmas tree lights, Rockefeller Center. **H1 31**

New Year's Eve celebrations, Times Sq.   **F6 31**

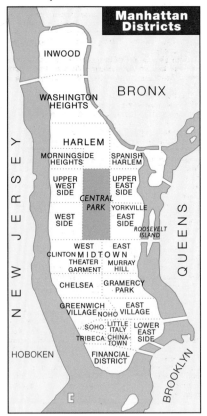

Manhattan Districts

THE METROPOLITAN MUSEUM OF ART

See Map 27 square H1

The Metropolitan, with the Louvre in Paris, the Prado (Madrid), the Heritage (St. Petersburg) and the British Museum, is one of the greatest museums in the world today, attracting large crowds, all eager to see its panoramic collection of arts and cultures from all parts of the globe from prehistory to the 20th century.

The idea of a National Museum of Art was conceived in 1886 in Paris by a caucus of American artists and patrons led by John Jay - the grandson of the first Chief Justice of the United States. Before the museum had found a home it had acquired its first collection. The city legislature then raised $500,000 to construct a building for the museum on Fifth Avenue facing Central Park. The small red bricked Neo-Gothic building was finished in 1880, and the growing collection including 175 paintings, mostly Dutch and Flemish, helped the museum become established. The original building by Calvert Vaux was soon engulfed by the museum's constant expansion; what with new wings and the re-orientation of the building to face out on Fifth Avenue, the original structure is now only partially visible through the glass atrium pyramid of the Lehman Wing.

Although overall a rich melange of architectural styles, the Fifth Avenue frontage is a majestic sight. The Central Pavilion and the Great Hall - one of New York's great interior spaces - were designed by Richard Morris Hunt and finished on his death by his son. The facade is in the Beaux-Arts style and has three wide bays flanked by Corinthian columns, with an attic elegantly trimmed with female masks set against scallop shells. The disconcerting feature is the stacked blocks of uncut stone on top of the columns: these entablatures were to be topped by sculpture groups, but the Trustees were unenthused. The blocks were placed there anyway, hoping to force the Trustee's hand, but they have remained uncut to this day.

In the following years under the financier and benefactor J. P. Morgan's direction the museum broadened the European collection, and by 1906 had begun its Egyptian excavations. For many years the Met rejected the tenets of modern art, especially abstraction, and thus spurned acquiring modern American and European art.

Today the Met has over three million objects in its collection, with too many must-sees to list. But highlights include: a three-room temple - The Temple of Dendur (ca 15 BC) built by a Roman emperor and lifted from Lower Nubia (where it would have been lost in the Aswan Dam) in 1965 and reconstructed faithfully at the Met - most evocative at night when floodlit. The museum's Egyptian collection is second only to the one in the Cairo museum.

Of special interest to keyboard players is the Musical Instrument's gallery which contains the oldest piano in existence today. The Asian rooms have some beautiful porcelain pieces, while the large assemblage of over 2000 European paintings is not to be missed. Look out for the *View of Toledo* by El Greco, Jan van Eych's *Dyptych*, *The Grand Canal* by Turner, *Portrait of a Man* by Franz Hals, and the last study by Seurat for *A Sunday on La Grande Jatte,* the small *Journey of the Magi* by Sasseta, and the happy art of Auguste Renoir. Also here you will find Cézanne, Manet, Monet, Rembrandt, Pissaro, Van Gogh, and many many more.

In the American Wing you will discover the famous painting of *Washington Crossing the Delaware* by Leutze and the heroic landscape *The Rocky Mountains* by Albert Bierstadt, there is also a living room by the architect Frank Lloyd Wright as featured in one of his prairie houses, and some exquisite glass by Louis Tiffany.

The Portrait of Gertrude Stein by Picasso is located in the Twentieth Century Gallery.

The Costume Institute and Photograph Gallery will both stimulate your interest - see Edward Steichen's wonderfully moody *The Flatiron.*

Be warned, because of legalities concerning some of the collections acquired, many periods of art and certain artists' works are not always placed together. It may seem strange to single out the Met's museum store for mention, but The Shop is amazing. It contains the usual reproductions in the form of books, posters and calendars, but it also sells a remarkable range of statuary, porcelain, jewelry, Tiffany panes, pillboxes and much more.

A floor plan is available in the Great Hall where you will find an International Visitors desk where maps, brochures, and assistance are available in a variety of languages.

FIRST FLOOR
The American Wing - Arms & Armor - Arts of Africa - Oceania and the Americas - Egyptian Art - Greek and Roman Art - European Sculpture and Decorative Arts - Grace Rainey Rogers Auditorium - Medieval Art- Robert Lehmann Collection - 20th Century Art - The Museum Restaurant - Museum Cafeteria - Museum Bar and Cafe.

SECOND FLOOR
The American Wing - Ancient Near Eastern Art - Asian Art - Chinese Art - Japanese Art - Islamic Art - Drawings, Prints and Photographs - European Paintings - Greek and Roman Art - 19c European Paintings and Sculpture - Musical Instruments - 20th Century Art - South and Southeast Asian Art - The Great Hall Balcony Bar
ROOF SCULPTURE GARDEN
Well worth a visit for the views of Manhattan (open seasonally and weather permitting).
Museum closed on Mondays.
Suns, Tues -Thurs 09.15 - 17.15,
Friday and Saturday 9.30-20 45 Suggested Charge
THE CLOISTERS, a museum of medieval art and architecture in Fort Tryon Park at the northern tip of Manhattan, is part of the Met, and one admission ticket allows entrance to both on the same day. If you can manage to visit both, I would suggest, start at the Cloisters - a peaceful less crowded place, picnic in the park, where you have some fine views (especially in autumn) across the Hudson river, and then return by bus number 4 which will take you door to door.

See Page 9 for the opening hours.

MUSEUMS AND ART GALLERIES

ABIGAIL ADAMS SMITH MUSEUM   **E1 33**
421 East 61 Street. Standing almost in the shadow of the meccano-like structured Queensboro Bridge, this former coach house was built in the Federal style. It was part of a much grander residence which was burnt down in 1826, and then converted into a tavern - the Mount Vernon Hotel. The collection of 18c-19c artefacts and furniture is displayed in nine period rooms surrounded by a neat formal garden.
Monday - Friday 12.00 -16.00, Suns 13.00 - 17.00,
Closed Saturdays and August   *Charge*

AFRICAN ART. MUSEUM OF   **H6 39**
593 Broadway. A small intimate colorful museum situated in SoHo, exhibiting traditional and contemporary African art treasures and culture: masks, paintings, sculptures, performances and films.   *Suggested Charge*
Tues - Fris 10.30 - 17.30, Sats & Suns 12.00 - 18.00

AMERICAN CRAFT MUSEUM   **H3 31**
40 West 53rd Street. A modern museum (1986) with an atrium and a swirling stairwell. Although somewhat sparsely displayed, it showcases: fiber arts, fabrics, glass, ceramics, metalwork, etc.
Weds - Suns 10.00 - 17.00, Tuesday 20.00   *Charge*

AMERICAN FOLK ART. MUSEUM OF   **D6 26**
2 Lincoln Center. This gallery is located near the Metropolitan Opera House. Exhibits range from 18th century to contemporary art forms: carved-wood animals, Navajo rugs, paintings, sculptures.
Tuesday to Sunday 11.00 -19.30 Suggested Charge

AMERICAN INDIAN. NAT. MUS. of the   **D4 46**
1 Bowling Green. The Heye Center (part of the Smithsonian Institute) in the old U.S. Custom Building is where you will find this interesting museum that contains the largest collection of Indian art in the world. Encompassing the rich and varied cultures of North and South America ranging from 3200 BC to the present day. Headdresses, clothes, silverwork, blowguns, and possessions of the great chiefs Geronimo and Crazy Horse. Music and dance presentations.
Daily 10.00 - 17.00   *Free*

AMERICAN MUSEUM of the MOVING IMAGE
Kaufman - Astoria Studios 35th Avenue, Queens. Housed on three floors in an old Paramount movie studio, a part of which became in 1988 the nation's only film and television museum. Take the R Train to Steinway Street (Steinway pianos are still made nearby) and walk two blocks south and turn right. *Beau Geste* was made in Queens and artists like Rudolph Valentino, Gloria Swanson, the Marx Brothers, Woody Allen and Bob Fosse all made films here. The museum, perhaps not as large as you might have anticipated, features: props, costumes, cameras, a wonderful collection of posters, original sets and memorabilia. There are clips of directors explaining their art; and classic films in the Riklis Theater on a rotating basis. Look out for the fun mirror that changes your appearance, making you the star!   *Charge*
Tues - Fris 12.00 - 16.00, Sats & Suns 12.00 -18.00

AMERICAN MUSEUM OF NATURAL HISTORY
Central Park West   **E2 27**
Yes the one in *On the Town* where they danced and collapsed the dinosaur skeleton. Be selective for this is an extensive museum. First get a free floor plan from the information desk.
Starting at the top - the Fourth Floor - you will find the refurbished dinosaur collection complete with interactive displays. The Third Floor is partly given over to the Hall of Primates which plots the

evolution and development of man: also you will find a diorama featuring a 10-foot Komodo dragon in the Hall of Reptiles and Amphibians. Arriving at the Second Floor central rotunda you are greeted by Barosaurus the 50-foot-high herbivore from the Jurassic period - well over 140 million years ago! In the People Center are artefacts and artworks illustrating and exploring the history of the world. On the First Floor suspended above your head in the Hall of Ocean Life is a replica of a leviathan - the greatest of all animals - the 94-foot-long Blue Whale. The Hall of Minerals and Gems is where you can view *The Star of India,* the largest blue sapphire in the world; perhaps even more amazing is the four-and-a-half-billion-year-old meteorite *Agnighito* recovered from Greenland.
Sunday to Thursday 10.00 - 17.45,
Friday and Saturday 10.00 - 20.45 Suggested Charge
The Imax Theater projects nature's phenomena onto a four-story-high screen every hour on the half hour, double features are presented Fridays and Saturdays at 18.00 and 19.30.   *Charge*
The Hayden Planetarium
Entrance is through the museum or 81st Street. Astronomical information and marvelous space and sky theaters that will make you and your children's minds boggle!   *Charge*
Shows October to June, Mons - Fris 13.30 -16.30.
Saturday 11.00 - 17.00, Sunday 11.00 - 16.00.
July to Sept. as above except Sats, Suns 12.00 - 16.00

ASIA SOCIETY GALLERY   **B4 28**
725 Park Avenue. A permanent exhibition of sculptures, bronzes, ceramics, etc., bought by John Rockefeller on his travels across the continents. Worth a visit if any of the temporary exhibitions excite you.   *Tuesday - Saturday 11.00 - 18.00,*
Friday 20.00, Sunday 12.00 - 17.00   *Charge*

BARRIO. EL MUSEO DEL   **A1 24**
1230 Fifth Avenue. This is the museum for the art, history and culture of not only Puerto Rico but all Latin American countries. It plays an important part in the community of El Barrio (Spanish Harlem). Displays of modern paintings, sculptures, photographs, etc; as well as artefacts from the Taínos who inhabited the Caribbean area between 1000 and 1500 AD.   *Weds - Suns 11.00 - 17.00*
May to Sept. Thurs 12.00 - 19.00 Suggested Charge

BLACK FASHION MUSEUM   **F1 21**
155 West 126th Street. Situated in Harlem in a terraced brownstone house with exhibits that change every six months. It features costumes designed by Blacks: some from theater and films and others that go back to the eighteenth century.
Daily 12.00 - 20.00   *Suggested Charge*

CITY OF NEW YORK. MUSEUM of the   **A1 24**
Fifth Avenue at 103rd Street. All the exhibits on view in this Neo-Georgian building are used to illustrate the history of New York from inception to the present day. There are period rooms, costumes, dolls houses, paintings, maps, models, and always changing exhibitions which I have no doubt you will find extremely interesting. Broadway is depicted with posters, music, and a survey of theatrical productions from 1886 to the present day.   *Wednesday to Saturday 10.00 - 17.00*
Sundays 13.00 - 17.00   *Suggested Charge*

CLOISTERS. THE
Fort Tryon Park. This museum is a branch of the Metropolitan and a single fee buys admission to both on the same day. As the title suggests it resembles a medieval monastery. Although it was

constructed between 1934 and 1938, many parts date from the 12th-15th century and were brought from France and Spain and re-assembled. I live in St. Albans in England, and some of this architecture would not look out of place in our ancient Abbey and Cathedral, which is a mixture of styles as many monasteries were in the Middle Ages.

Perhaps the rich 16th-century Unicorn Tapestries woven in Brussels are the museum's most famous possession. There are also illuminated manuscripts, a gilt Monkey Cup and a complete set of 15th-century playing cards - one of the earliest in existence. Outside the flower and herb gardens are planted with species grown in medieval times. On a fine day many will find the trip to the Cloisters memorable for the walk through Fort Tryon Park and the lovely views (see Page 7).

Take the A train to 190 Street station, walk through the park, or catch Bus No. 4 which will take you outside the entrance and return to the Metropolitan.

March to October, Tuesday to Sunday 9.30 - 17.15.
Nov. to Feb. 9.30 - 16.45   *Suggested Charge*

COOPER - HEWITT MUSEUM   A5 24

2 East 91st Street. The National Design Museum, part of the Smithsonian Institute, located in the 1901 mansion of the philanthropist Andrew Carnegie: he gave away over $280 million, mostly to build hundreds of libraries. The museum always has imaginative themed exhibitions, and amongst the holdings are: wallpaper, textiles, jewelry, porcelain and a large collection of architectural drawings.

Wednesday - Saturday 10.00 - 17.00, Tuesday 21.00,
Sundays 12.00 - 17.00   *Charge*

ELLIS ISLAND IMMIGRATION MUSEUM

Until 1954 this was the reception area for millions of immigrants. When you look through the windows of the waiting room you can imagine how they must have been inspired by the vision of Manhattan. The trip to the island is all about their agony and ecstasy: many families had experienced tragedy even before arrival. The mortality rate on some of the ships was very high in the early days. The bronze statue of Annie Moore arriving from Ireland in 1892 says it all. To reach the island buy your ferry tickets at Castle Clinton (C5 46) - the round trip will take you to the Statue of Liberty as well. Ferries run from Battery Park every 30-45 minutes beginning at 9.15.

Ticket and Schedule Information ring   *269 5755*

FRAUNCES TAVERN MUSEUM   D4 46

54 Pearl Street. The very edge of Manhattan - the embankment - ran along Pearl Street where you will find this elegant Georgian style - partly re-constructed - 18th-century tavern. Who cares if it is not completely the original, it certainly has the atmosphere! George Washington did frequent the tavern and his farewell speech was delivered on this site. The Hogarth caricatures in the Lafayette room also add to the period authenticity.

Monday to Friday 10.00 - 16.00
Closed Saturdays and Sundays   *Charge*

FRICK COLLECTION   A4 28

1 East 70th Street. Henry Frick was a steel magnate, a millionaire before he was thirty, and this mansion was built in 1914, five years before he died. Unusually relaxing for a museum, it has a luxurious interior, gardens, and an internal glass-covered courtyard where the sound of water can be heard springing from a central fountain into a pool. Essentially a collection of old masters: Vermeer, Gainsborough, Reynolds, Boucher, Rembrandt, El Greco are all on view here. Of special interest is a self-portrait of Franz Hals and *Sir Thomas More* by Holbein. There are also paintings by Turner and Whistler and some exquisite Limoges enamels.   *Charge*

Tues - Sats 10.00 - 18.00, Sundays 13.00 - 18.00

GUGGENHEIM MUSEUM. Solomon R.   A5 24

1071 Fifth Avenue. The only important building to be seen in New York designed by the great architect Frank Lloyd Wright, it has stood like a tornado amongst the mansions of Park Avenue since it was erected in 1959. A recent addition, a nine-story tower annex was constructed using Wright's original scheme as a blueprint. It has now doubled the exhibition space. When you saunter down (as you should) the revolving ramp of the rotunda you can now access the new galleries of the tower. Dedicated to displaying 19c-20c art - the architecture and the impressionist and post-impressionist masterpieces attract large crowds. Among the colorful exhibits are works by: Degas, Gauguin, Manet, Toulouse-Lautrec, Van Gogh, Cézanne, Chagall, Picasso, Klee, Delauney, Modigliani, Léger and sculptures by the marvelous Constantin Brancusi. Famous for its Wassily Kandinsky collection this landmark is well worth visiting. On Fridays those on limited budgets may prefer to go between 18.00 and 20.00 when you pay what you wish!

Sunday - Wednesday 10.00 - 18.00,
Friday and Saturday 10.00 - 20.00   *Charge*

GUGGENHEIM MUSEUM SoHo   F1 43

575 Broadway. This downtown annex in a historic 19c loft building features special exhibitions that are complementary to the main museum. In the basement is *Time for T*, a cafe and emporium with reputedly New York's largest selection of teas.

Sunday, Wednesday and Friday 11.00 - 18.00
Saturday 11.00 - 20.00   *Charge*

INTERNATIONAL CENTER of PHOTOGRAPHY

1130 Fifth Avenue and   A4 24
1133 Avenue of the Americas   G6 31
Manhattan's only museum devoted exclusively to photography. The principal building is a Neo-Georgian mansion on Fifth Avenue. Both places have excellent displays by the great journalist photographers.

Tues - Suns 11.00 - 18.00, Tuesday 20.00   Charge

JAPAN SOCIETY GALLERY   D5 32

333 East 47th Street. Close to the United Nations building, the society holds changing exhibitions illustrating Japanese life, culture and art. There is an auditorium and occasionally there are screenings of major Japanese classic films by directors such as Kurosawa, etc.   *Students Free*

Tuesday to Sunday 11.00 - 17.00. Suggested Charge

JEWISH MUSEUM   A4 24

1109 Fifth Avenue. Using art and artefacts, 4000 years of Jewish history are born again in this Gothic-styled chateau. In 1993, with help from some of the masons working on St. John the Divine in Harlem, it was extended and renovated. On display are cups, lamps, manuscripts, a mosaic wall from Persia and works of art including paintings by Marc Chagall.

After 5pm Tuesday entrance is free.

Mons, Weds, Thurs, Suns 11.00 - 17.45
Tuesdays 11.00 - 20.00   *Charge*

LOWER EAST SIDE TENEMENT Museum B2 44

97 Orchard Street. An eye-opener, a tenement building dating from 1863 in the heart of an area which once was the center for the clothing industry. Here new immigrants were crammed in conditions worse than any other place on earth. The museum and tour capture the drama of the immigrant experience. There are also guided tours of the neighborhood.   Box Office 90 Orchard Street.

Tuesday - Friday 12.00 - 17.00,
Saturday and Sunday 11.00 - 17.00   *Charge*

MODERN ART. MUSEUM OF   H3 31
11 West 53rd Street. The concept behind MoMa is to relate the course of modern visual arts from the late 19th century onwards. You can view photography by Eugène Atget, who recorded old Paris as it was changing just before the First World War; contrast this with the Surrealist photo art of Man Ray whose paintings are also displayed. On this Second Floor there are many treasures of modern art, for example: Cézanne's *Le Baigneur,* Van Gogh's *Starry Night* with its turbulent sky, a panoramic canvas by Monet in the *Water Lilies* series, *Zapatistas,* a resolutely powerful picture by Mexico's José Orozco, *Les Demoiselles d'Avignon,* the painting by Picasso that initiated Cubist art, and the Surrealist horizon of Dali's *Persistence of Memory.* The sculpture of Constantin Brancusi is here also: see his simple and effective *Bird in Space,* with its reflective metal surface leading your eyes upwards. Other artists represented here are: Seurat, Bonnard,Toulouse-Lautrec, Miró, Léger, Klimt, etc. The Third Floor contains Pop-Art and more recent paintings: Warhol, Rauschenberg and Francis Bacon are here for you to analyse. Continue upwards to the Fourth and Top Floor where there are architectural models and designs including mass-produced objects and posters.
When you return to the Ground Floor grab a chair and rest in the open air Sculpture Garden or perhaps continue down to the Basement which has two movie-theaters - admission price includes entrance to the shows.   *Saturday to Tuesday 11.00 - 18.00*

NATIONAL ACADEMY OF DESIGN   A5 24
1038 Fifth Avenue.   A changing exhibition of paintings, sculptures, prints and drawings in a Beaux-Arts town house. Famous for American art and portraits in particular, there are examples of the art of John Singer Sargent, Winslow Homer, etc. As you enter you see the statue of *Diana* by Anna Huntington: her *Joan of Arc,* an equestrian statue, proudly faces Riverside Park (see B4 22).
Weds - Suns 12.00 - 17.00, Fris 20.00   *Charge*

NICHOLAS ROERICH MUSEUM   B6 20
319 West 107th Street. Not a well-known museum but worth seeking out. Nicholas Konstantin Roerich was a Russian painter and philosopher. A brilliant colorist, he was responsible for the décor of Diaghilev's Ballet Russe production of *Prince Igor;* subsequently he worked with Stravinsky on the libretto of the *Rite of Spring,* for which he also designed the scenery. Later in life he travelled to the Himalayas, eventually settling in the Punjab valley where he made over 500 paintings. He died in 1947 and this museum is dedicated to informing people of his ideas through his writing and painting. Worth looking for are two paintings, *Kanchenjunga* and *Mother of the World.* There are also Sunday concerts.   *Tuesday to Sunday 14.00 - 17.00.*   *Free*

PIERPOINT-MORGAN LIBRARY   B2 36
29 East 36th Street. A superb collection housed in a Roman-style palazzo. It consists of manuscripts, drawings, rare books and documents acquired by a financier and founder of the YMCA, J. P. Morgan. The library's interior is incredibly rich and it holds many priceless articles: the first printed book - the *Gutenberg Bible* - scores by Mozart, Beethoven and Mahler, and a perfect copy of Sir Thomas Malory's *Morte d'Arthur* printed by Caxton. *Suggested Charge*
Tues - Sats 10.30 - 17.00, Sunday 13.00 - 17.00

POLICE ACADEMY MUSEUM   B1 40
235 East 20th Street. A violin case containing a tommy gun, memories of the Prohibition Era, uniforms and badges dating back to 1845.
Monday to Friday 9.00 - 14.00   *Charge*

SCHOMBURG CENTER
Subway Line 2 or 3 to 135 Street or Bus 7 or 102. 515 Lenox Avenue, Harlem. A research library for black culture established by Arthur Schomburg, a Puerto Rican of African origin. Contains books, photographs, recordings and works of art. The theater is well known for its jazz concerts.   *Free*
Mons - Weds 12.00 - 20.00, Fris - Sats 10.00 - 18.00

SEA-AIR-SPACE MUSEUM. INTREPID   A5 30
Pier 86 West 46th Street. Launched into action in World War II in 1942, *Intrepid* is an aircraft carrier - a survivor of a kamikaze attack. Aboard *Intrepid* are fighter planes, wonders of the space age, models, the original Iwo Jima monument and a Panavision screen. Other ships and helicopters are also here on short term display. The sights and sounds *Intrepid* endured during history's largest naval battle will take you into the battle zone! A major addition is the *Guadalcanal,* a US Navy helicopter carrier also used as a heliport for sightseeing tours.   *Charge*
Summer Daily 10.00 -17.00, and Winter Weds - Suns.

SOUTH STREET SEAPORT MUSEUM   F2 47
The eight-block historic seaport district celebrating New York's maritime past, when South Street was known as the Street of Ships. A good place to shop, eat superb seafood or listen to music - a very pleasant place indeed, but it does not recreate the atmosphere of the original port at all, so look at the photographs! Basically an open museum and shopping center. Admission allows entrance to the galleries, tours and historic vessels. Harbor cruises on sailing ships are extra.   *Daily 10.00 - 17.00*

STUDIO MUSEUM IN HARLEM   F1 21
144 West 125th Street. A bright cultural center for local, national, African and Afro-Caribbean art, that features paintings, sculptures, photographs, and temporary exhibitions. *Weds - Fris 10.00 - 17.00 Saturday and Sunday 13.00 - 18.00.*   *Charge*

TELEVISION AND RADIO. MUSEUM OF   H4 31
25 East 52nd Street. An incomparable collection of broadcasting archives is here for your education and pleasure. Your selection from the computerized catalogue relays to the librarian, then you go to a console room to watch or listen, perhaps to a 30's broadcast, a sports program or the last episode of a series you missed - whatever did happen to the Fugitive?
Tues - Suns 12.00 - 18.00, Thurs 20.00   *Charge*

THEODORE ROOSEVELT BIRTHPLACE   H1 39
28 East 20th Street. The original brownstone house was demolished and this is a replica. Teddy was born on this site in 1858, and is renowned for his Rough Riders and his exploits in the Spanish-American War. As President McKinley's vice president he became the first and only New Yorker so far to achieve the presidency after McKinley was assassinated in 1901.
Wednesday to Sunday 9.00 - 17.00   *Charge*

WHITNEY MUSEUM of AMERICAN ART B3 28
945 Madison Avenue. The museum of 20th-century American art, and as you might expect incarcerated in a Legoland-like building that almost topples over you. Although the museum has no permanent displays certain artists' works are always on view. Hunt out the flower paintings of Georgia O'Keeffe, the boxing painting *Dempsey and Firpo* by George Bellows, the wistful art of Edward Hopper and Stuart Davis's clever and colorful abstract designs. There is also an annex in the Philip Morris building (B2 32) close by Grand Central Station - useful if you have to kill some time waiting for a train.The museum, famed for its Biennial Exhibition, never ceases to be controversial and attracts large crowds.
Wednesday to Sunday 11.00 - 18.00   *Charge*
Students note that Thursdays 18.00 -20.00 it is free.

PLACES OF INTEREST

ACTORS STUDIO   **D6 30**
432 West 44th Street. The Method School founded in 1947, and since 1955 occupying this painted brick church by the Theater District. Elia Kazan, Marlon Brando, Shelley Winters, Al Pacino have all been associated with this group which was under the artistic direction of Lee Strasberg until he died. Films like Kazan's *On the Waterfront* made across the Hudson in Hoboken, New Jersey, are the culmination of the 'method style'. Productions and script readings can be viewed by appointment. Phone: *757 0870. Monday - Friday 9.00 - 17.00*

BRIDGES
Brooklyn Bridge see Page 50.
George Washington Bridge
Anchored into a rocky cliff on the New Jersey side and spanning 1068 meters of the Hudson River, it is the only bridge linking N.J. to Manhattan. Constructed in 1931, a lower level was added 31 years later: the original idea by the architects Cass Gilbert and Othmar Ammann for the towers to be enclosed in granite in the Beaux-Arts style was abandoned because of the Depression. Probably best viewed on a Circle Line boat trip it rises 64.6 meters above the river and quite justly it is a greatly admired and influential bridge. If you walk across the bridge you can get straight onto a walking path in NJ's Palisades Park. Take the A train to 181st Street or buses 4, 5 or 100 to the George Washington Bridge Bus Station.
Manhattan Bridge   **D5 44**
Accessed on the Manhattan side through a Beaux-Arts colonnade which could be enhanced with some attention to the surrounding area. This suspension bridge was built in 1909 and takes a great deal of traffic, both cars and subway trains. It also has a pedestrian walkway connecting to Brooklyn.
Queensboro Bridge   **F2 33**
The bulk of web-like ironwork make this two-level cantilevered bridge not the most attractive to be seen in New York. Constructed in 1909, it straddles Roosevelt Island linking Manhattan to Queens.
Triborough Bridge   **H1 25**
Precisely what the name implies : a three-pronged viaduct-bridge structure finished in 1936 and linking the three boroughs, Manhattan, Queens, and Bronx.
Williamsburg Bridge   **G1 45**
Opened in 1903, twenty years after the Brooklyn Bridge, is was the second bridge to span the East River. At the time it linked Manhattan with the city of Williamsburg (now integrated into Brooklyn), and created a pathway from the tenements.
Verrazano Narrows Bridge
Spanning 'The Narrows' (the New York Harbor entrance) between Brooklyn and Staten Island this suspension bridge was designed by Othmar Ammann and opened in 1964. The toll plaza on Staten Island is the scene of the start of the NYC Marathon, which follows a route across the bridge and through Brooklyn. Suspended from four steel wire cables (diameter: 91 centimeters) the bridge has two levels - for traffic only!

CASTLE CLINTON National Monument C5 46
Built as a gunnery in 1811 for protection against a British invasion: it stood ninety meters offshore. Never used for this purpose it became a theater, the Castle Garden, where P.T. Barnum introduced his *Swedish Nightingale* Jenny Lind. From 1855 to 1892 it was used for immigration, then for an aquarium. Today it is integrated into Battery Park. You can purchase tickets for the Statue of Liberty -Ellis Island boat trips here. *Daily 8.30 - 17.00 Free*

CHURCHES OF INTEREST
John Street Methodist   **D2 46**
44 John Street. In the heart of the financial district and built of brownstone in 1841 in the Italianate style. Inside the door is the figure of Peter Williams, a slave freed by the congregation; later he established closeby a black Methodist church. Historical objects and prints can be viewed.
Riverside Church   **B2 20**
Riverside Drive. A 1930 skyscraper Gothic-Revival church with a tower 392-foot-high enclosing a steel frame and a stunning five-octave carillon with a 20-ton bass bell (the heaviest ever cast). Wagner lovers will recognize the clock-tune as the Holy Grail motif from *Parsifal*. Renowned for its stained glass windows which originate from Belgium, the church finds a great deal of its inspiration from Chartres Cathedral. To reach the observation deck for the panoramic views buy an elevator ticket. The final stairway has open vents, so choose your day!
St.Bartholomew's Episcopal   **B4 32**
Park Avenue.   An ornate domed Byzantine-style church with a terrace garden - an oasis in mid Manhattan. The salmon pink bricks appear to match and contrast with the neighboring General Electric building. The front Romanesque portal belonged to the previous church on this site.
St.John the Divine see Architecture Page 50
St.Mark's in the Bowery   **B3 40**
Second Avenue.   The resting place of Peter Stuyvesant and his family, on ground which was once part of his estate. Built in 1799 with additions: the 1828 Greek Revival steeple and more recently - after a fire - some abstract stained glass windows in the balcony.
St.Patrick's Cathedral see Architecture Page 51
St.Paul's Chapel   **D1 46**
Broadway. The oldest church and pre-revolutionary building in Manhattan, and if proof is needed - George Washington had a pew here in the north aisle. It reminds one of St.Martin's in London; the spire and portico, later additions, evoke the resemblance. The entrance in fact is not the Broadway end, but through the historic churchyard: while in this peaceful haven look for the 'Actors Monument' in the center, a donation from a fellow thespian, Edmond Kean. The chapel today is famous for its Waterford crystal chandeliers and its classical music concerts.
Trinity Church   **C3 46**
Broadway. Looking down Wall Street since 1846 in the labyrinth of high finance is the Gothic spire of this famous church: for fifty years the tallest building in Manhattan. After taking in the spire look at the great bronze doors and then walk around the churchyard where you will find the monument to steamboat inventor Robert Fulton. One donation to build the original church on this site came from the pirate Captain Kidd: today he might have found some kindred spirits in the shadows of Wall Street.
FEDERAL HALL National Memorial   **D3 46**
28 Wall Street. A Doric columned temple, fronted by the statue of George Washington on the spot where he was inaugurated in 1789. Inside is a museum and visitor information center.
Monday to Friday 9.00 - 17.00   *Free*
GRACIE MANSION   **F5 25**
Carl Schurz Park. A balconied country house (1799) in the Federal style: the official residence of New York's mayor since 1942 and Fiorello La Guardia's office. For guided tours ring *570 4751*.   *Charge*
Mid March to mid October, Wednesday 10.00 - 15.00

GRANT'S TOMB   A2 20
Riverside Drive. On a hilltop that overlooks the Hudson River is the largest mausoleum in the US. It contains the remains in black sarcophagi of Ulysses S. Grant and his wife surrounded by busts of his comrades at arms. The son of an Ohio farmer, Grant went to West Point and later became the commander of the Union army in the Civil War, and later the 18th president of the United States. A trip to the tomb will fill you in with his exploits and history and you can see the photographs as well. Who knows whether he deserves such a monument: the black community of Harlem nearby certainly would not see him as their saviour, he was on the right side though!
Wednesday - Sunday 9.00 - 17.00   *Free*

NEW YORK STOCK EXCHANGE   D3 46
8 Broad Street. As you view the front of this 1903 building from Wall Street, the columns and the pediment seem very theatrical, and yet you know this is an important place - the nerve center of capitalism - Dow Jones averages! The visitors' center is located at 20 Broad Street and is where to obtain free viewing tickets, but try to arrive before midday. The enclosed gallery where you can watch the proceedings is on the third floor and overlooks the trading floor. Do you remember those films of ticker-tape parades going down lower Broadway? This is where the paper came from.
Monday to Friday 9.30 - 16.00   *Free*

ROCKEFELLER CENTER   G4 31
The greatest buiding complex in Manhattan and mostly built between 1931 and 1939, it contains: offices, cafes, restaurants, the NBC broadcasting studios, Radio City Music Hall, an ice-skating rink , a fountain, shops, boutiques, and the famous Rainbow Room in the RCA (now General Electric) building - the flagship of the center. The decorations in and outside the buildings are superb, full of Art Deco works by the greatest of 20th-century artists and sculptors: like *Atlas* (H4 31) by Lee Lawrie, a work that enhances and combines perfectly with the architecture. Arriving from Fifth Avenue along the Channel Gardens, you overlook the fountain with the golden *Prometheus* by Paul Manship: not an elegant work, yet undeniably striking; although at first glance it does not seem well proportioned, it is!

JERSEY CITY

HUDSON RIVER

MANHATTAN

BROOKLYN BRIDGE

BATTERY PARK

EAST RIVER

ELLIS ISLAND

LIBERTY ISLAND

GOVERNOR'S ISLAND

BROOKLYN-BATTERY TUNNEL

UPPER NEW YORK BAY

BROOKLYN

STATEN ISLAND FERRY

0	KILOMETRES	4
0	MILES	2

ROOSEVELT ISLAND Aerial Tramway   D2 32
A glide across the East River on this Swiss-style aerial tram, featured in many films since it opened in 1976, is the most interesting way to reach the two-mile-long island. A great place for a walk, it is virtually traffic free, although it does have an internal bus service. Not far from the Meditation Steps (G6 29), where you can sit and watch the river, there is an original 1796 farmhouse - Blackwell House - and if you walk to the northern tip there are gardens and picnic areas. At the southern end of the island the proposed Franklin D. Roosevelt memorial will be built - across the river from the United Nations. A feature of Roosevelt I. is the rubbish collection system servicing most buildings, whisking away rubbish 55mph along tunnels to the AVAC building (H3 29) where it is compacted to one-fifth its size.
Subway tokens can be used for the aerial ride which operates every fifteen minutes.

STATUE OF LIBERTY
The symbol not only of New York but of the whole of the United States. The statue was a gift from France in 1886 to commemorate the French and American revolutions. The monument contains work of the best in their vocations: the pedestal is by Richard Morris Hunt, the engineering by Gustave Eiffel and the sculpting by Auguste Bartholdi. The statue was built in Bartholdi's Paris studio, then shipped in pieces to New York: the outer skin of 2.5mm copper sheets encases Eiffel's iron skeleton. Elevators take you to the top of the plinth, then it is a climb inside the statue up and down two staircases - not for the faint of heart. To get an idea of the view the great liners had entering the harbor, the cheap way is to take the Staten Island Ferry - the best value in NYC - 50 cents round trip! Pay at the Staten Island end on your return. Although Liberty is depicted as a woman, it was thirty-four years after the inauguration ceremony that women were allowed to vote in America.
Tickets for the ferry (include entry to Liberty and Ellis Islands) obtainable in Battery Park at the ticket booth in Castle Clinton (C5 46) 8.30 - 16.30.
Daily 9.30 - 17.00, July and August 9.00 - 18.00. Departures are every 30 minutes both ways.

TIMES SQUARE   F6 31
Not a square at all, an intersection, named after *The New York Times* whose offices are still nearby. This is the very heart of the Theater District and arguably the city center, lit with dozens of colorful neon signs. The place to view the news zipper and the Sony Jumbotron is from the comfort of the Marriott Marquis lounge bar. To me the square still has an element of Runyon magic about it.

UNITED NATIONS   E6 33
Forgetting the noble purpose of the buildings, they are not attractive. One man, John D. Rockefeller Jr., donated the site worth $8.5 million at the time, 1946. The Secretariat, a glass skyscraper, unusually for Manhattan standing free with space around, is mundane, inside and out. Proving that politicians in committees are not great judges of art and aesthetics. If you decide to take a tour, you will see the General Assembly and Security Council chambers and this is where the buildings succeed most.   *Daily tours 9.15 - 16.45 are every 45 minutes. Closed January and February weekends.*

WASHINGTON SQ. Memorial Arch   G4 39
In 1889 a wooden arch was erected on this former parade ground for the celebrations remembering George Washington's inauguration. It was received with such enthusiasm that a modified stone version was erected in 1895. The two figures on each side are both Washington: as General with the figures of Fame and Valour and as the first President with Wisdom and Justice. The square is famed for its twice yearly Open Air Art Exhibition.

SHOPPING

More than in any other city in the world, in New York, shopping is necessary sight-seeing. A visit to Macy's and to the glamorous emporia of Fifth Avenue is as essential as the view from the Empire State. There are seven world-class department stores, and branches of most major designers, many clustered near Fifth Avenue and 57th Street. From the 60's upwards Madison Avenue is lined with boutiques, shops and galleries with the highest price tags in the city. Columbus Avenue offers boutiques and women's fashions with modest prices, and SoHo is the home of the cutting edge designers and boutiques catering to the young and fashionable. For all-American affordable fashions, branches of The Gap are everywhere, and there are particularly large ones with children's departments on Broadway at 42nd Street and at 34th Street.

The Department Stores

BARNEY'S   Down E2 39 - Uptown B1 32
The ground-floor boutiques set the style of the shops. Look for the jewelry glittering in the tropical fish tank. The layout of the upper floors can be confusing, but there is a dizzying selection of men's clothing in particular, and the tailoring is first rate.
BERGDORF GOODMAN   A2 32
Shop here for top names, classy atmosphere, and excellent service. Don't miss the Kentshire Antiques Room for antiques and estate jewelry on the seventh floor, with its intimate scale and gorgeous view of Central Park. The designer men's clothes are housed in a separate building across the street.
BLOOMINGDALES   C2 32
This is New York's trend-setting store. Although pricey, with a combination of the house label and clothes of famous designers, good sales put Bloomie's in reach of the everyday shopper.
CENTURY 21   C1 46
For something completely different: no elegant building, no special services, just steeply discounted brand-name merchandise in 16 departments. The store is near Wall Street and opens at 7.45am, for the best bargains get there early before the crowds.
HENRI BENDEL   A2 32
The whimsical department store and my favorite. Bendel's stock is well selected rather than deep: witness the wonderful (tiny) hat department on the atrium level. The use of blond wood and black-gold balcony railings in the interior, and René Lalique windows on the facade, creates an air of elegance and festivity.
LORD and TAYLOR   H1 35
Although it has other good departments, this is the place to shop for bargains in women's clothes. It specializes in American designers, and its seasonal dress sales are hard to beat. The Christmas windows are award-winning.
MACY'S   G3 35
Founded in 1858, Macy's is the largest department store in the world. They say if you haven't seen Macy's you haven't seen New York. Macy's invented the Christmas-themed window in 1874, and provided the Santa of *The Miracle on 34th Street*. At Easter the flower displays are gorgeous.
SAKS FIFTH AVENUE   A4 32
Saks is housed in an elegant 1924 building with Rockefeller Center and St. Patrick's Cathedral as its neighbors. The stock is comprehensive and tasteful and the staff knowledgeable.

Art and Antiques

ART   There are hundreds of art galleries in Manhattan, many of which carry art of museum quality, from Old Masters to Andy Warhol, which you are free to browse without making a six-figure purchase. The *Art Now Gallery Guide* is free at most galleries and lists exhibits monthly, and both the *New Yorker* and *New York Magazine* list gallery highlights. The neighborhoods to browse are Upper Madison Avenue in the Seventies; 57th Street east and west of Fifth Avenue, particularly the Fuller building at 41st East 57th ; and in SoHo (where art tends to be modern and contemporary), along West Broadway and Greene Street south of Houston, and Prince Street between Greene Street and Broadway.
New York also offers a chance to visit one of the world's preeminent auction houses, such as **Christie's** (B2 32) and **Sotheby's** (E4 29). The contents of a sale are usually on display for browsing a couple of days before the sale.
ANTIQUES The highlights of New York antiquing is the Winter Antiques Fair at the Seventh Regiment Armory (B5 28). There is no special antique row like some cities, however the tri-level Manhattan Art and Antiques Center (D3 32) is the largest of its kind in the United States, and has over 100 small galleries.
Daily 10.30 - 18.00, Sunday 12.00 - 18.00.

Markets

FLEA MARKETS New York doesn't have the established markets of Paris and London, but there are many weekend flea markets and street vendors who set up along busy shopping streets on weekends; for instance, Broadway just north of Houston. Two established flea markets are:
The Annex Antique Fair   G5 35
Sixth Avenue between 24th and 27th Streets.
Sats and Suns with Sunday flea market.
Intermediate School 44   D3 26
Columbus Av. between 75th and 76th Street. *Sunday.*

GREENMARKETS Farmers from several states belong to the Greenmarket organization that brings fresh produce, cheese, fruit and home-baked goods to markets around the city. The most established of these is the Union Square Greenmarket (H2 39) which is held on *Wednesday, Friday and Saturday*

FISH and FLOWER MARKETS These are wholesale markets more for tourist viewing than buying and only for the early riser. The Flower Market, (G4 35) runs from 26th to 30th Street between Sixth and Seventh Avenues in the very early morning - get there by 7.00 am at the latest. The Fulton Fish Market, (F2 47) at South Street Seaport runs from midnight to 8.00am.

> **GOURMET GROCERS** These shops may not have the splendor of Harrod's but they do offer a vast array of the freshest select produce. **Balducci's** (F4 39) in the village boasts fine meats and delicacies and superb cheeses. **Dean & De Luca** (F1 43) on Broadway in SoHo excels with delicious prepared foods. **Grace's** (C4 28) offer exotic imports. **Zabar's** (C2 26) is the New York institution, filled with intense Upper West siders elbowing for the best selection of gourmet food in the city.

JAZZ IN NEW YORK

New Orleans, Chicago, Los Angeles, and Kansas City have all been cultural backgrounds for jazz. But all routes lead eventually to New York. Six years before the first black band was recorded, the Original Dixieland Jassband made the first jazz recordings in NYC in 1917. By the early 30's Louis Armstrong and Duke Ellington were in Manhattan. Duke was living in Edgecombe Avenue, Sugar Hill, and playing the Cotton Club in Harlem to strictly white audiences. Prohibition (repealed in 1933) had brought after-hours clubs - where musicians played for fun: instrumentalists with virtuosity like Artie Shaw. They learnt jazz while making a living in the orchestras of the radio networks that were centered in Manhattan. It was only when backed by John Hammond (who was related to the Vanderbilts) and with the magnificent Fletcher Henderson arrangements that Benny Goodman played Carnegie Hall in 1938 and jazz became legitimate. In no other city anywhere was jazz more concentrated; as styles developed they co-existed alongside each other. Bebop was born at Minton's Playhouse West 118 Street: Charlie Parker and Dizzy Gillespie gave the music form. The Apollo Theater (E1 21) in Harlem launched many careers - Ella Fitzgerald for one, and the incomparable Billie Holiday, sang there too.

Because so many clubs were clustered along 52nd Street, it became known as Swing Street, and today the sidewalk insertions remind us of the legends. **The City Voice** Jazz resounds every night all over Manhattan, and even Carnegie Hall has its own band led by the trumpet player Jon Faddis. The Tavern on the Green (F5 27) in Central Park will provide most tourists with an enjoyable evening; Woody Allen will make you grin when he blows his clarinet at Michael's Pub (C3 32). My advice is to pick up a copy of *Hot House* at Tower Records or HMV's, or the *Village Voice* to see who is playing where. Aficionados will drift towards Greenwich Village where there are many famous clubs. The acoustic mecca is the Village Vanguard (E3 39) where the great Bill Evans, Miles Davis, John Coltrane and Art Pepper had their performances recorded for posterity; close by is Sweet Basil (E5 39), respected for its artists and continental cuisine. Bradley's (H3 39) is a great piano bar with wood-panelled walls which create a warm ambience - the piano, a bequest, belonged to Paul Desmond! The Blue Note (F5 39) always has top artists: if you can't get in, a few yards away is my favorite, Visiones (G5 39), reasonably priced, good food (Spanish cuisine) and a magnificent nine-foot grand piano. For tropical cuisine and Latin sounds - samba, salsa, etc. - S.O.B.S. (F6 39) is the venue. Other venues are The Knitting Factory (F4 43), Iridium (E1 31) and Birdland (C6 30) - now near its original location.

FAMOUS RESTAURANTS AND BARS

You need not wait until night falls to experience the delights that await you in New York's restaurants, especially if you are off to the theater in the evening. The best bargains can be had by ordering the prix fixe lunch menu when dinner might break the bank. Many of the city's finest restaurants are located midtown. Lutèce (D4 32) is a bastion of classic French cuisine with enchanting decor and an indoor garden. At Le Cirque (B6 28), a stylish whimsical place with fittings to match, a French/Italian cuisine is served. The'21' Club (H4 31), a Prohibition era classic has a top-quality American menu with a 50,000-bottle wine cellar. The Four Seasons (B4 32), located in the Seagram Building, is ravishingly elegant with tables set around a square pool. Patsy's (F3 31) is alleged to have been Frank Sinatra's favorite Italian restaurant in NYC.
But some of the best dining establishments are to be found in decidedly unstuffy neighborhoods. Bouley (E4 43) is an unlikely Provençal fantasy in the bleak warehouse-lined streets of fashionable Tribeca. Close by is the Tribeca Grill (D4 42) inhabited by Manhattan's film colony - Robert De Niro is joint owner. The Gotham Bar and Grill (G3 39) is quintessentially New York modern from the decor to the cutting edge cuisine. The excellent Union Square Cafe (H2 39) is a hot spot for the very cool, serving up creative Italian and American to the downtown and literary sets. In Yorkville, Elaine's (D5 24) is the place to dine with celebrities. For the best soul food and barbecue try Sylvia's (G1 21) up in Harlem, it's worth the trip!
For a slice of New York tradition, The Oyster Bar beneath Grand Central Station (B6 32) is a must. Whether in the tiled low-vaulted saloon or the dining room, you may choose from a vast seafood menu including a dozen varieties of fresh oysters.

An evening of romance or celebration should take you to the dazzling Tavern on the Green (F5 27) in Central Park, where a million fairy lights twinkle on the surrounding trees. For an evening of elegant dining and dancing, there is only one place, The Rainbow Room (H4 31) at the very top of the RCA (now General Electric) building, where the view is as intoxicating as the wine. The only restaurant to rival it is the River Cafe (A2 48) which is tucked almost under the Brooklyn Bridge, and from where the Manhattan skyline is no less than breathtaking.
I am sure you won't want to go glamorous at every meal. How about a classic New York Jewish deli (which does not guarantee Kosher) for an enormous corned beef or pastrami sandwich or perhaps a reuben? The Carnegie Deli (F3 31) and the Stage Delicatessen (F3 31) can be found in the West Fifties. On the Lower East Side and somewhat cheaper is Katz's (D6 40) in an authentic location - you might meet Sally! Not in this category really is the Harley Davidson Cafe (G3 31), a draw for easy riders and lovers of the great machine - my grandad had one of the first exported to England. At Fraunces Tavern (D4 46) you get the feeling for history, the Revolution and George Washington. Pete's Tavern (A1 40) dates from 1874 and is New York's oldest continuously operating pub. In Greenwich Village Ye Waverly Inn (E3 39) is an old converted carriage house dating from 1844. The Village has so many very reasonably priced good restaurants I am sure you will find some place that suits your requirements. Another area to mention is South Street Seaport (F2 47) where you can dine 'al fresco' enjoying the freshest seafood available. Finally the Nirvana Penthouse (H2 31) has some spectacular views over Central Park while serving you zesty Indo-Bengali cuisine. Bon appetit!

SERVICES AND USEFUL INFORMATION

Information Centers

N.Y. CONVENTION & VISITORS Bureau   **E2 31**
2 Columbus Circle   © *(212) 397 8722*
Open from Monday to Saturday   9.00 - 18.00
    and Sundays and Holidays   10.00 - 15.00
For 24hr information © *toll free 1-800-NYC-VISIT*
Information and advance reservations   press 1
Visitors Publications   press 2
Information and Activities   press 3
Multilingual Counselors   press 4

Emergency Services

FIRE - MEDICAL - POLICE   Dial 911
HOSPITALS All hospitals have emergency rooms,
and any treatment will have to be paid for. All
major credit cards are accepted.
DOCTORS ON CALL
Hotel or home visits   © *(718) 238 2100*
DENTAL emergency treatment   © *679 3966*
PHARMACIES Duane Reade is the chain drugstore
and they are like most pharmacies open from
Monday to Saturday 9.00-18.00, Sunday times vary.
24hr PHARMACY   © *755 2266*
Kaufman, 557 Lexington Avenue at 50th Street.
POST OFFICES On weekdays they open 9.00-17.00
and usually on Saturdays from 9.00 until midday.
Stamps can be bought from some supermarkets
and shops although they are cheaper at post offices.
24 HOUR POST OFFICE   **E3 35**
General Post Office, Eighth Avenue.
LOST PROPERTY New York is not the best place
to retrieve anything. However you might be lucky if
you try the NYC Transit Authority, located at the
34th Street/Penn Station (E3 35), for anything lost
on the Subway or Buses. Or call © *718 625 6200*
Mons, Weds, Fris 8.00 - 12.00, Thurs 11.00 - 18.45
If it is lost other than on the transport system go
to your nearest police precinct - see map.

TELEPHONE   To make an international call
dial 011 then the country code - Australia 61,
Ireland 353, United Kingdom 44, and then the
area code followed by the individual number.
NATIONAL HOLIDAYS New Year's Day, Martin
Luther King Jr. Memorial Day (3rd Monday in
Jan.), Presidents' Day (3rd Monday in Feb.),
Memorial Day (last Monday in May), Independence
Day (4th July), Labor Day (1st Monday in Sept.),
Columbus Day (2nd Monday in Oct.), Veterans'
Day (Nov. 11th), Thanksgiving (3rd Thurs in Nov.),
Christmas Day (25th December).
BANKING HOURS   Banks usually open from
Monday to Friday 9.00 - 15.30. Some open on
Saturdays from 9.00 to midday.
Thomas Cook traveler's checks are not easy to
cash at some banks, nevertheless they will probably
accept a few. Get a list of offices before you arrive.
The Times Square office opens Monday to Saturday,
9.00 - 19.00. If you cannot reach this one,
© dial *1 800 CURRENCY.*
American Express is the most widely accepted
Traveler's Check.
SUBWAY   Open entrances are recognized by
Green globes - a Red globe means a restricted
entrance. Buy a pack of tokens, they can be used
on the buses as well.
BUSES Fares are a flat rate, use subway tokens
or the exact change - no notes! If you need to
change buses to go across town ask for a transfer
ticket when you pay your fare: this is valid for
one hour on any connection. Most buses operate

between 7.00 and 22.00. You can recognize the
stops by the yellow-painted curbs and signs near
to corners.
TAXIS They are vacant when the number on the roof
is lit up. If you cross the river you pay the tolls as
well. Always ask for a receipt which can be easily
printed out. The recognized tip is about 15%.
AIRPORT TRANSFERS A free bus takes you from
any terminal to the Howard Beach/JFK airport
subway station where you can take the A train
into Manhattan - this is the cheapest way. I
recommend (if you cannot afford a taxi) the Carey
Airport Express bus which leaves every 30 minutes
and drops you at Grand Central Station or the
Port Authority Bus Terminal (E1 35) where a cab
ride could take you to your hotel if the bus is not
going there - it does go to some hotels.
To get from La Guardia Airport the Carey bus is
also a lot cheaper than a taxi.
If you arrive at Newark Airport, this is served by
the New Jersey Transit bus which takes you to the
Port Authority Bus Terminal (E1 35).
On your return journey your hotel clerk can often
procure a cheap taxi for you by sharing!

Boat Trips

There are many trips: you can spend a whole day
going up the Hudson or just take the 90-minute
harbor cruise with NY Waterway. Then there is
the famous Circle Line trip around Manhattan
Island which takes three hours. On a late summer
evening their Harbor Lights cruise is ideal too.
Nothing anywhere is better value than the Staten
Island Ferry trip: 50 cents there and back and it
operates 24 hours a day, see Page 12.
Circle Line   **A6 30**
Pier 83, West 42nd Street   © *563 3200*
NY Waterway   **A2 34**
12th Avenue   © *800 533 3779*
World Yacht (Dinner Cruises)   **A1 34**
Pier 81, West 41st Street   © *929 7090*

Helicopter Flights

An unbelievable spectacle if you can afford it:
hovering around the Manhattan skyscrapers.
Flights are from 9.00 - 21.00.
Liberty Helicopters   **A4 34**
Heliport, 12th Av. and West 30th St. © *967 6464*
Island Helicopter   **E3 37**
Heliport, East 34th Street   © *683 4575*

CLOTHING and SHOE SIZES approximate						
SHIRTS						
Europe	36	37	38	39	40	41	42
UK and USA	14	14.5	15	15.5	16	16.5	17
DRESSES						
Europe	36	38	40	42	44	46	48
UK	8	10	12	14	16	18	20
USA	6	8	10	12	14	16	18
MEN'S SHOES						
Europe	39	40	41	42	43	44	45
UK and USA	6	7	7.5	8.5	9	10	11
WOMEN'S SHOES						
Europe	35.5	36	36.5	37	37.5	38	39
UK	3	3.5	4	4.5	5	5.5	6
USA	4.5	5	5.5	6	6.5	7	7.5

LEGEND - ENGLISH - FRANÇAIS - DEUTSCH - NEDERLANDS - ITALIANO - ESPAÑOL

HOSPITALS
Hôpitaux
Krankenhäus
Ziekenhuisen
Ospedali
Hospitales

Bellevue Hospital Center

TOURIST INFORMATION
Informations Touristiques
Touristenauskünfte
Toeristen Informatie
Informazione Turistiche
Información Turistica

POLICE PRECINCT
Gendarmerie
Polizeiwache
Politie
Polizia
Comisaría

FOOTPATH
Sentier
Fusspfad
Voetpad
Sentiero
Senda

POST OFFICE
Bureau de Poste
Postamt
Postkantoor
Ufficio Postale
Correos

PUBLIC PARK
Jardin Public
Öffentliche Parkanlage
Publiek Park
Giardino Pubblico
Parque Publico

PHARMACY
Pharmacie
Apotheke
Apotheek
Farmacia
Farmácia

CEMETERY
Cimetière
Friedhof
Begraafplaats
Cimiteri
Cementerio

HOTEL
Hôtel
Hotel
Hotel
Albergo
Hotel

ALGONQUIN ■

OUTDOOR STATUES and SCULPTURES *Hare on Bell*
Statues et Sculptures dehors
Im Freien stehende Standbilder und Skulpturen
Standbeelden en Beeldhouwkunst buiten
Statue e Sculture all'aperto
Estatura y Escultura al fresco

CHURCH OF SPECIAL INTEREST
Églises intéressants
Sehenswerte Kirchen
Interassant Kirken
Chiese di Interesse
Iglesias de Interes

RIVERSIDE CHURCH †

THEATRES and CONCERT HALLS
Théâtres et Salles de Concerts
Theater und Konzertsäle
Theaters en Concertzalen
Teatri e Sale dei Concerti
Teatros y Salas de Concertos

NEW ■
AMSTERDAM

SYNAGOGUE
Synagogue
Synagoge
Synagogen
Sinagoga
Sinagoga

✦

CINEMA
Cinéma
Kino
Bioscoop
Cinema
Cine

ZIEGFELD ■

JAZZ CLUB
Jazz Club
Jazz Club
Jazz Club
Jazz Club
Jazz Club

VISIONES ★

RESTAURANT, CAFE or BAR
Restaurant, Café ou Bar
Restaurant, Cafe oder Bar
Restaurant, Café of Buffet
Ristorante, Cafe o Bar
Restorant, Cafe o Bar

Tribeca Grill ●

DISCO or DANCE HALL
Disco ou Salle de Danse
Disko oder Tanzsaal
Disco of Dans Zaal
Disco o Sala di Danza
Disco o Salón de Baile

Roseland ★

CABARET
Cabaret
Kabarett
Cabaret
Cabaret
Cabaret

RAINBOW AND STARS ■

SUBWAY STATION
Station de Métro
U-Bahnstation
Ondergrondse Station
Stazione di Metropolitana
Estación de Metro

42 Street Ⓢ

RAILWAY STATION
Gares
Bahnhof
Station
Stazione
Estación

GRAND CENTRAL STATION ≫

INTERCHANGE STATION
Station de Correspondance
Umsteigestation
Aansluiting op andere Lijnen
Station di coincidenza
Correspondencia

Ⓢ

MARKET
Marché
Markt
Markt
Mercato
Mercado

Ⓜ

Ⓡ RESTROOM - TOILET - BATHROOM   Toilette Toilet Toeletta Retrete

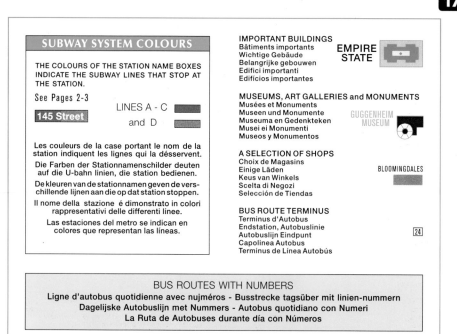

SUBWAY SYSTEM COLOURS

THE COLOURS OF THE STATION NAME BOXES
INDICATE THE SUBWAY LINES THAT STOP AT
THE STATION.

See Pages 2-3

145 Street LINES A - C
and D

Les couleurs de la case portant le nom de la
station indiquent les lignes qui la désservent.

Die Farben der Stationnamenschilder deuten
auf die U-bahn linien, die station bedienen.

De kleuren van de stationnamen geven de vers-
chillende lijnen aan die op dat station stoppen.

Il nome della stazione é dimonstrato in colori
rappresentativi delle differenti linee.

Las estaciones del metro se indican en
colores que representan las líneas.

IMPORTANT BUILDINGS
Bâtiments importants
Wichtige Gebäude
Belangrijke gebouwen
Edifici importanti
Edifícios importantes

EMPIRE STATE

MUSEUMS, ART GALLERIES and MONUMENTS
Musées et Monuments
Museen und Monumente
Museuma en Gedenkteken
Musei ei Monumenti
Museos y Monumentos

GUGGENHEIM MUSEUM

A SELECTION OF SHOPS
Choix de Magasins
Einige Läden
Keus van Winkels
Scelta di Negozi
Selección de Tiendas

BLOOMINGDALES

BUS ROUTE TERMINUS
Terminus d'Autobus
Endstation, Autobuslinie
Autobuslijn Eindpunt
Capolinea Autobus
Terminus de Línea Autobús

24

BUS ROUTES WITH NUMBERS
Ligne d'autobus quotidienne avec nujméros - Busstrecke tagsüber mit linien-nummern
Dagelijkse Autobuslijn met Nummers - Autobus quotidiano con Numeri
La Ruta de Autobuses durante día con Números

BUS ROUTES in GREY
Arrows indicate BUSES in one direction only.

Lignes d'autobus en GRIS. *Les flèches indiquent
les lignes d'autobus dans un seul sens.*

GRAUE busstrecken.
Pfeile zeigen auf Busverkehr nur in Pfeilrichtung.

Autobuslijnen in GRIJS.
Pijlen geven de bussen aan alleen in één direktie.

Linee di Autobus in GRIGIO.
Le frecce indicano autobus in una sola direzione.

Ruta autobús en GRIS.
Las flechas indican la ruta de los autobuses en una sola dirección.

1 3 4
19

BUS ROUTE NUMBERS are indicated in
the border.

Les lignes dépassant les bordures de la
carte sont indiquées en marge.

Buslinien-Nummern sind am
Kartenrand angegeben.

Bus route nummers zijn aangegeven
in de kantlijn.

I numeri delle linee di autobus
son indicate sul margine.

Los números de autobús se indican
en el margen.

approximately 6 inches to 1 mile
1 CENTIMETRE TO 100 METRES

SCALE

300 METRES EQUAL 328 YARDS

ENGLISH — The maps are divided into 300 metre squares with divisions of 100 metres indicated in the border.

FRANÇAIS — Les cartes sont divisées en carrés de 300 mètres de côté, avec divisions de 100 mètres indiquées en bordure.

DEUTSCH — Die karten sind in karrees von 300 quadratmeter unterteilt 100-Meter-Unterteilung ist am Rand markiert.

NEDERLANDS — De kaarten zijn verdeeld in vierkanten van 300 meter met verdelingen van 100meter in de kanlijn.

ITALIANO — Le mappe sono suddivise in 300 metri quadrati con divisione di 100 metri indicate nel margine.

ESPAÑOL — Las cartas están divididas en cuadrados de 300 metros, con divisiones de 100 metros indicados en el margen.

METRES

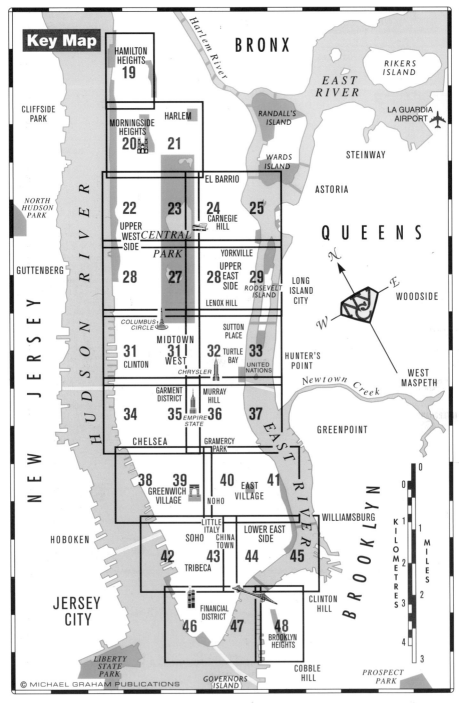

Key Map

HAMILTON HEIGHTS
19

BRONX

Harlem River

RIKERS ISLAND

EAST RIVER

LA GUARDIA AIRPORT

CLIFFSIDE PARK

MORNINGSIDE HEIGHTS
20

HARLEM
21

RANDALL'S ISLAND

WARDS ISLAND

STEINWAY

ASTORIA

EL BARRIO

NORTH HUDSON PARK

22

23

24 CARNEGIE HILL

25

QUEENS

UPPER WEST SIDE

CENTRAL PARK

YORKVILLE

GUTTENBERG

28

27

28 UPPER EAST SIDE

29 ROOSEVELT ISLAND

LONG ISLAND CITY

WOODSIDE

LENOX HILL

COLUMBUS CIRCLE

MIDTOWN WEST

SUTTON PLACE

HUNTER'S POINT

WEST MASPETH

31 CLINTON

31

32 TURTLE BAY

33 UNITED NATIONS

CHRYSLER

Newtown Creek

GARMENT DISTRICT

MURRAY HILL

34

35 EMPIRE STATE

36

37

GREENPOINT

CHELSEA

GRAMERCY PARK

38

39 GREENWICH VILLAGE

40

EAST VILLAGE

41

WILLIAMSBURG

NOHO

LITTLE ITALY

HOBOKEN

SOHO

CHINA TOWN

LOWER EAST SIDE

42

43

44

45

TRIBECA

CLINTON HILL

JERSEY CITY

FINANCIAL DISTRICT

46

47

48 BROOKLYN HEIGHTS

BROOKLYN

LIBERTY STATE PARK

GOVERNORS ISLAND

COBBLE HILL

PROSPECT PARK

NEW JERSEY

HUDSON RIVER

EAST RIVER

0
KILOMETRES
MILES

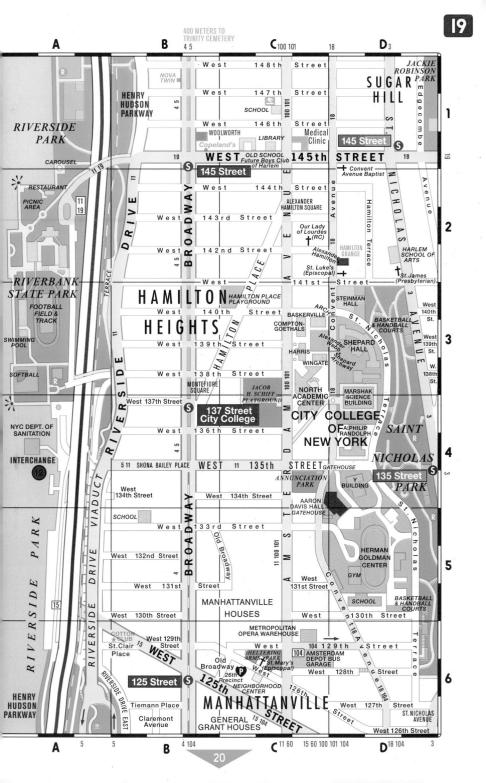

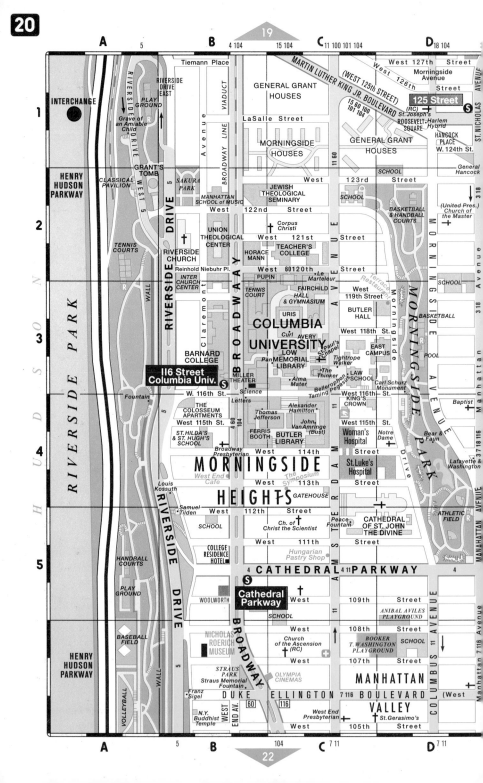

A   5   **B**   4 104   15 104   **C** 11 100 101 104   **D** 18 104

Tiemann Place

West 127th Street

West 126th

Morningside Avenue

INTERCHANGE

RIVERSIDE DRIVE EAST

PLAY GROUND

GENERAL GRANT HOUSES

MARTIN LUTHER KING JR. BOULEVARD

(WEST 125th STREET)

15 60 100 101 104

125 Street

Grave of an Amiable Child

LaSalle Street

St. Joseph's (RC)

ROOSEVELT SQUARE

Harlem Hybrid

1

GRANT'S TOMB

MORNINGSIDE HOUSES

GENERAL GRANT HOUSES

11 60

HANCOCK PLACE

W. 124th St.

General Hancock

HENRY HUDSON PARKWAY

CLASSICAL PAVILION

SAKURA Park

West 123rd Street

SCHOOL

318

2

TENNIS COURTS

MANHATTAN SCHOOL of MUSIC

West 122nd Street

JEWISH THEOLOGICAL SEMINARY

SCHOOL

(United Pres.) Church of the Master

UNION THEOLOGICAL CENTER

Corpus Christi

West 121st Street

TEACHER'S COLLEGE

BASKETBALL & HANDBALL COURTS

RIVERSIDE CHURCH

Reinhold Niebuhr Pl.

HORACE MANN

West 60 120th St.

Le Marteleur

SCHOOL

INTER CHURCH CENTER

PUPIN

West 119th Street

Terrace Restaurant

318

3

TENNIS COURT

FAIRCHILD HALL & GYMNASIUM

BUTLER HALL

BASKETBALL

BARNARD COLLEGE

URIS

COLUMBIA UNIVERSITY

Curl

AVERY

St. Paul's Chapel

West 118th St.

EAST CAMPUS

POOL

116 Street Columbia Univ.

LOW MEMORIAL LIBRARY

Pan

Tightrope Walker

LAW SCHOOL

Carl Schurz Monument

MILLER THEATER

'The Thinker'

Bellerophon Pegasus

Baptist

W. 116th St.

Science

Alma Mater

Taming

West 116th St.

KING'S CROWN

Letters

Fountain

THE COLOSSEUM APARTMENTS

Thomas Jefferson

Alexander Hamilton

West 115th St.

Woman's Hospital

Notre Dame

Bear & Faun

4

West 115th St.

FERRIS BOOTH

John Van Amringe (Bust)

Lafayette & Washington

ST. HILDA'S & ST. HUGH'S SCHOOL

BUTLER LIBRARY

Broadway Presbyterian

West 114th Street

St. Luke's Hospital

MORNINGSIDE

Louis Kossuth

West End Cafe

West 113th Street

The Symposium

GATEHOUSE

ATHLETIC FIELD

HEIGHTS

Samuel Tilden

West 112th Street

Ch. of Christ the Scientist

Peace Fountain

CATHEDRAL OF ST. JOHN THE DIVINE

5

HANDBALL COURTS

SCHOOL

West 111th Street

Hungarian Pastry Shop

COLLEGE RESIDENCE HOTEL

PLAY GROUND

4 **CATHEDRAL** 4 11 **PARKWAY** 4

WOOLWORTH

Cathedral Parkway

West 109th Street

SCHOOL

ANIBAL AVILES PLAYGROUND

BASEBALL FIELD

NICHOLAS ROERICH MUSEUM

West 108th Street

Church of the Ascension (RC)

BOOKER T. WASHINGTON PLAYGROUND

SCHOOL

STRAUS PARK

Straus Memorial Fountain

West 107th Street

HENRY HUDSON PARKWAY

VOLLEYBALL

Franz Sigel

N.Y. Buddhist Temple

60

DUKE **ELLINGTON** 7 116 **BOULEVARD**

OLYMPIA CINEMAS

116

MANHATTAN

West 105th Street

West End Presbyterian

St. Gerasimo's

VALLEY

(West

A   5   **B**   104   **C** 7 11   **D** 7 11

RIVERSIDE PARK

HUDSON

RIVERSIDE DRIVE

BROADWAY

AMSTERDAM AVENUE

Morningside Drive

MORNINGSIDE PARK

MANHATTAN AVENUE

COLUMBUS AVENUE

ST. NICHOLAS AVENUE

West 127th Street Langston Hughes Pl. LANGSTON HUGHES LIVED HERE

MASONIC TEMPLE

BLACK FASHION MUSEUM

Sylvia's

Mt. Moriah (Baptist)

West 126th Street

HARLEM STATE OFFICE BUILDING

East 126th St.

APOLLO THEATRE

VICTORIA 5

Sydenham Clinic

125 Street Ⓢ

Baptist House of Prayer

NATIONAL BLACK THEATRE

FIFTH AFRICAN SQ.

MARTIN LUTHER KING JR. BOULEVARD (WEST 125th STREET) (EAST 125th St.)

15 60 100 101

MART 125

THERESA TOWERS

Refuge Temple

STUDIO MUSEUM IN HARLEM

Lenox Lounge

15 60 100 101

WEST 124th ST. EAST 124th ST.

West 124th Street

(7th Day Adventist) Ephesus

Ethiopian Hebrew

SWIMMING POOL

Diving Pool

E. 123rd St.

HANCOCK PARK

P 28th Precinct

West 123rd Street

MOUNT MORRIS PARK HISTORIC DISTRICT

Bethelite Community (Baptist)

MARCUS GARVEY

3 18

West 122nd Street

(Episcopal) St.Martin's

PARK

Fire Watchtower (1856)

E. 122nd St.

CHILDREN'S CENTER

SCHOOL

West 121st Street

Mt. Morris (Presbyterian)

RECREATION CENTER & AMPHITHEATER

E. 121st St.

West 120th Street

Mt.Olivet (Baptist)

WEST 120th ST. EAST 120th ST.

HARLEM

West 119th Street

5th Avenue Hideway

FIFTH

East 119th

2nd St.John Baptist

Bethel Way of the Cross

ST. NICHOLAS

West 118th Street

FREDERICK DOUGLASS

St.Thomas the Apostle (RC)

Faith Mission

East 118th St.

West 117th Street

A. PHILIP RANDOLPH SQUARE

East 117th

NEW YORK'S FIRST MOVIE PALACE

116 Street Ⓢ

First Corinthian (Baptist)

WEST 116th STREET 102 116 EAST 116th ST.

St. Stephen's Ⓢ

116 Street

SAMUEL MARX TRIANGLE

Memorial Baptist

Malcolm Shabazz Mosque

East 116th

LIBRARY

West 115th Street

All Souls

East 115th

HIGH SCHOOL

West 114th Street

PLAY GROUND

MARTIN LUTHER KING JUNIOR TOWERS

ROBERT A.TAFT HOUSES

Jehovah's Witness

West 113th Street

FIRE STATION

SCHOOL

West 112th Street

SCHOOLS

East 112th St.

NEW EBONY

West 111th Street

REV. JOHN LADSON PLACE

Emily's

La Hermosa

East 111th

(APARTMENTS) SCHOMBURG PLAZA

2 3 4 18

110 Street Central Park N.

DUKE ELLINGTON CIRCLE

EAST 110th St.

FREDERICK DOUGLASS CIRCLE

3 4 18

CENTRAL PARK NORTH

STRANGER'S GATE Ⓢ

PLAYGROUND

WARRIOR'S GATE

FARMER'S GATE

PIONEER'S GATE

18

Cathedral Parkway

MOUNTCLIFF ARCH

THE BLOCKHOUSE

THE CLIFF

DANA DISCOVERY CENTER

HARLEM MEER

East 109th St.

Southern Baptist

NORTH WOODS

WEST DRIVE

EAST DRIVE

East 108th St.

FIFTH AVENUE

1 2 3 4

06th St.)

GREAT HILL

SITE OF FORT CLINTON

East 107th St.

CENTRAL PARK WEST

R

CENTRAL

LOULA D. LASKER MEMORIAL RINK & POOL

East 106th St.

106

PARK

Untermeyer Fountain

East 105th St.

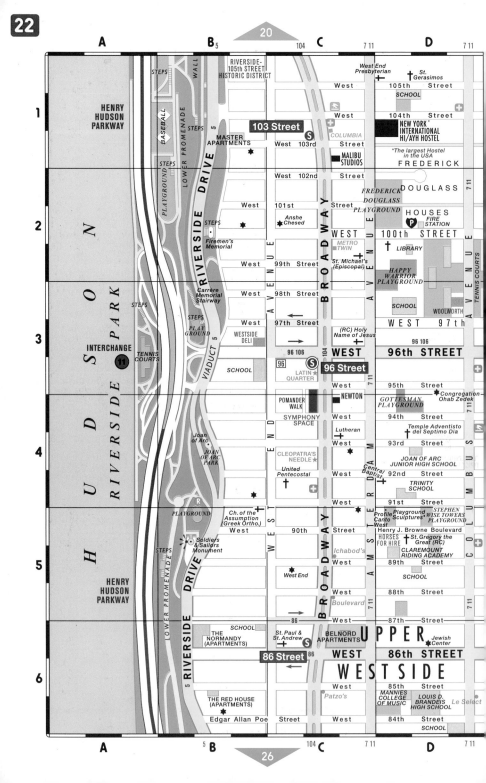

A   **B**   5   104   **C**   7 11   **D**   7 11

20

1

HENRY
HUDSON
PARKWAY

WALL

STEPS

BASEBALL

STEPS

STEPS

PLAYGROUND

LOWER PROMENADE

RIVERSIDE DRIVE

RIVERSIDE-
105TH STREET
HISTORIC DISTRICT

West End
Presbyterian

West   105th   Street

St.
Gerasimos

SCHOOL

West   104th   Street

103 Street Ⓢ

COLUMBIA

NEW YORK
INTERNATIONAL
HI/AYH HOSTEL

MASTER
APARTMENTS

West 103rd   Street

MALIBU
STUDIOS

*The largest Hostel
in the USA*

FREDERICK

2

West 102nd   Street

FREDERICK
DOUGLASS

DOUGLASS

West   101st   Street

FREDERICK
DOUGLASS
PLAYGROUND

HOUSES

P

FIRE
STATION

Firemen's
Memorial

Anshe
Chesed

STEPS

WEST   100th   STREET

METRO
TWIN

LIBRARY

West   99th Street

St. Michael's
(Episcopal)

HAPPY
WARRIOR
PLAYGROUND

TENNIS COURTS

N

RIVERSIDE PARK

HUDSON

Carrère
Memorial
Stairway

West   98th   Street

SCHOOL

WOOLWORTH

STEPS

West   97th   Street

(RC) Holy
Name of Jesus

WEST   97th

3

INTERCHANGE
11

TENNIS
COURTS

STEPS

PLAY
GROUND

VIADUCT 5

WESTSIDE
DELI

SCHOOL

96 106   WEST   96th STREET

96 106

96

96 Street Ⓢ

LATIN
QUARTER

NEWTON

West   95th   Street

Congregation
Ohab Zedek

POMANDER
WALK

GOTTESMAN
PLAYGROUND

Joan
of Arc

JOAN
OF ARC
PARK

SYMPHONY
SPACE

West   94th   Street

Lutheran

Temple Adventisto
del Septimo Dia

4

CLEOPATRA'S
NEEDLE ★

West   93rd   Street

JOAN OF ARC
JUNIOR HIGH SCHOOL

United
Pentecostal

Central
Baptist

West   92nd   Street

TRINITY
SCHOOL

R

West   91st   Street

STEPHEN
WISE TOWERS
PLAYGROUND

PLAYGROUND

Ch. of the
Assumption
(Greek Ortho.)

Profile
Canto
West

Playground
Sculptures

Henry J. Browne Boulevard

5

HENRY
HUDSON
PARKWAY

STEPS

LOWER PROMENADE

RIVERSIDE DRIVE

Soldiers
& Sailors
Monument

West   90th   Street

HORSES
FOR HIRE

St. Gregory the
Great (RC)

CLAREMOUNT
RIDING ACADEMY

Ichabod's

West   89th   Street

SCHOOL

West End

West   88th   Street

Boulevard

7 11

86

West   87th   Street

RIVERSIDE

5

SCHOOL

THE
NORMANDY
(APARTMENTS)

St. Paul &
St. Andrew

Ⓢ

BELNORD
APARTMENTS

86 Street 86

UPPER

Jewish
Center

6

WEST   86th   STREET

WEST SIDE

West   85th   Street

Patzo's

MANNIES
COLLEGE
OF MUSIC

LOUIS D.
BRANDEIS
HIGH SCHOOL

Le Select

THE RED HOUSE
(APARTMENTS)

Edgar Allan Poe   Street

West   84th   Street

SCHOOL

A   5 **B**   104 **C**   7 11 **D**   7 11

26

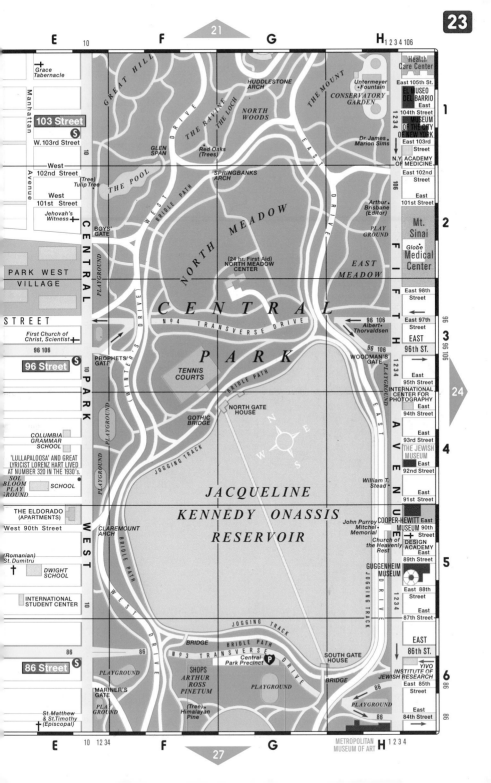

E   10   F   21   G   H 1 2 3 4 106

Grace Tabernacle

Health Care Center

East 105th St.

EL MUSEO DEL BARRIO East

104th Street

MUSEUM OF THE CITY OF NEW YORK

East 103rd Street

N.Y. ACADEMY OF MEDICINE

103 Street Ⓢ

W. 103rd Street

Manhattan

GREAT HILL

HUDDLESTONE ARCH

Untermeyer Fountain

CONSERVATORY GARDEN

THE MOUNT

THE RAVINE

THE LOCH

NORTH WOODS

Dr. James Marion Sims

D R I V E

West 102nd Street

(Tree) Tulip Tree

GLEN SPAN

Red Oaks (Trees)

SPRINGBANKS ARCH

THE POOL

BRIDLE PATH

East 102nd Street

106

West 101st Street

Jehovah's Witness

BOYS' GATE

N O R T H   M E A D O W

Arthur Brisbane (Editor)

PLAY GROUND

East 101st Street

2

Avenue

C E N T R A L

WEST

EAST

F

Mt. Sinai

PARK WEST VILLAGE

PLAYGROUND

(24 hr. First Aid) NORTH MEADOW CENTER

EAST MEADOW

Globe

Medical Center

S T R E E T

First Church of Christ, Scientist

96 106

C E N T R A L

DRIVE

N° 4   T R A N S V E R S E   D R I V E

F

F

East 98th Street

East 97th Street

96 106 Albert Thorvaldsen

EAST 96th ST.

96

96 106

96 Street Ⓢ

P A R K

10

PROPHETS' GATE

P A R K

WINTER'S

WOODMAN'S GATE

96 106

East 95th Street

3

1 2 3 4

East 94th Street

INTERNATIONAL CENTER FOR PHOTOGRAPHY

COLUMBIA GRAMMAR SCHOOL

PLAYGROUND

TENNIS COURTS

BRIDLE PATH

NORTH GATE HOUSE

PLAY GROUND

East 93rd Street

THE JEWISH MUSEUM East 92nd Street

4

A V E N U E

'LULLAPALOOSA' AND GREAT LYRICIST LORENZ HART LIVED AT NUMBER 320 IN THE 1930's.

GOTHIC BRIDGE

W N S E

W E S

SOL BLOOM PLAY GROUND   SCHOOL

PLAYGROUND

JOGGING TRACK

William T. Stead

East 91st Street

THE ELDORADO (APARTMENTS)

West 90th Street

CLAREMOUNT ARCH

J A C Q U E L I N E

John Purroy Mitchel Memorial

COOPER-HEWITT MUSEUM East 90th Street

(Romanian) St.Dumitru

DWIGHT SCHOOL

K E N N E D Y   O N A S S I S

Church of the Heavenly Rest

DESIGN ACADEMY East 89th Street

5

W E S T

BRIDLE PATH

R E S E R V O I R

GUGGENHEIM MUSEUM

East 88th Street

INTERNATIONAL STUDENT CENTER

10

WEST   DRIVE

JOGGING TRACK

1 2 3 4

East 87th Street

86

JOGGING   TRACK

EAST 86th ST.

86

86 Street Ⓢ

86

BRIDGE

BRIDLE PATH

N° 3   T R A N S V E R S E   D R I V E

Central Park Precinct Ⓟ

DRIVE

SOUTH GATE HOUSE

BRIDGE

YIVO INSTITUTE OF JEWISH RESEARCH

East 85th Street

6

86

PLAYGROUND

SHOPS ARTHUR ROSS PINETUM

PLAYGROUND

East 84th Street

MARINER'S GATE PLAY GROUND

St.Matthew & St.Timothy (Episcopal)

(Tree) Himalayan Pine

PLAYGROUND

86

E   10   12 34   F   27   G   METROPOLITAN MUSEUM OF ART   H 1 2 3 4

24

27

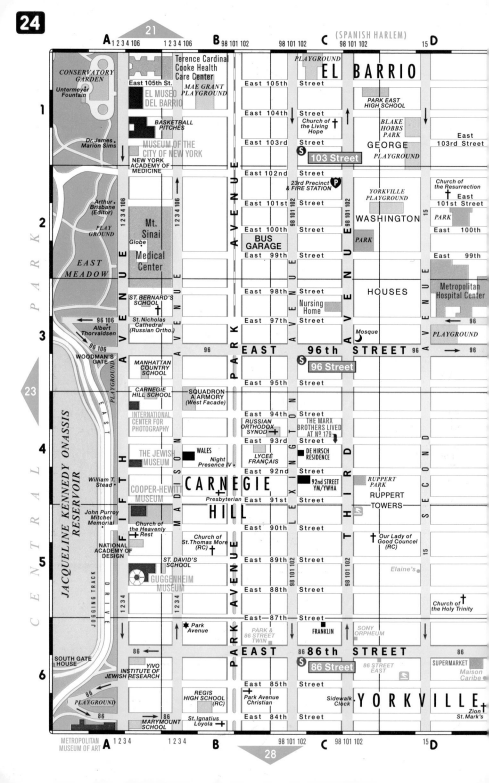

21

A 1 2 3 4 106   1 2 3 4 106   B 98 101 102   98 101 102   C (SPANISH HARLEM)   98 101 102   15 D

CONSERVATORY
GARDEN

Untermeyer
Fountain

East 105th St.

EL MUSEO
DEL BARRIO

Terence Cardinal
Cooke Health
Care Center

MAE GRANT
PLAYGROUND

PLAYGROUND

EL BARRIO

1

BASKETBALL
PITCHES

Dr. James
Marion Sims

MUSEUM OF THE
CITY OF NEW YORK

East 105th   Street

East 104th   Street

East 103rd   Street

PARK EAST
HIGH SCHOOL

BLAKE
HOBBS
PARK

Church of
the Living
Hope

GEORGE

East
103rd Street

NEW YORK
ACADEMY OF
MEDICINE

Ⓢ **103 Street**

PLAYGROUND

East 102nd   Street

Arthur
Brisbane
(Editor)

Mt.
Sinai

Globe

Medical
Center

23rd Precinct
& FIRE STATION Ⓟ

YORKVILLE
PLAYGROUND

Church of
the Resurrection
East
101st Street

PLAY
GROUND

East 101st   Street

WASHINGTON

PARK

2

EAST
MEADOW

East 100th   Street

BUS
GARAGE

East 99th   Street

PARK

East   100th

East   99th

ST. BERNARD'S
SCHOOL

East 98th   Street

HOUSES

Metropolitan
Hospital Center

Nursing
Home

St. Nicholas
Cathedral
(Russian Ortho.)

East 97th   Street

Mosque ☾

PLAYGROUND

← 96 106

Albert
Thorvaldsen

96 106

WOODMAN'S
GATE

96

EAST   96th   STREET   96 →   96

MANHATTAN
COUNTRY
SCHOOL

East 95th   Street

3

Ⓢ **96 Street**

CARNEGIE
HILL SCHOOL

SQUADRON
A ARMORY
(West Facade)

East 94th   Street

THE MARX
BROTHERS LIVED
AT N° 179

INTERNATIONAL
CENTER FOR
PHOTOGRAPHY

RUSSIAN
ORTHODOX
SYNOD

East 93rd   Street

WALES

THE JEWISH
MUSEUM

Night
Presence IV

LYCÉE
FRANÇAIS

DE HIRSCH
RESIDENCE

4

East 92nd   Street

CARNEGIE

92nd STREET
YM/YWHA

RUPPERT
PARK

William T.
Stead

COOPER-HEWITT
MUSEUM

Presbyterian

East 91st   Street

RUPPERT
TOWERS

HILL

John Purroy
Mitchel
Memorial

Church of
the Heavenly
Rest

East 90th   Street

NATIONAL
ACADEMY OF
DESIGN

Church of
St.Thomas More
(RC)

East 89th   Street

Our Lady of
Good Council
(RC)

Elaine's ●

5

ST. DAVID'S
SCHOOL

GUGGENHEIM
MUSEUM

East 88th   Street

Church of
the Holy Trinity

——— East—87th—— Street——

SOUTH GATE
HOUSE

★ Park
Avenue

PARK & 86
STREET
TWIN

FRANKLIN ■

SONY
ORPHEUM

86 ←

EAST   86   **86th   STREET**   86

YIVO
INSTITUTE OF
JEWISH RESEARCH

Ⓢ **86 Street**

86 STREET
EAST

SUPERMARKET

Maison
Caribe

6

PLAYGROUND

REGIS
HIGH SCHOOL
(RC)

East 85th   Street

Park Avenue
Christian

Sidewalk
Clock

YORKVILLE

86 →

MARYMOUNT
SCHOOL

St.Ignatius
Loyola

East 84th   Street

Zion
St. Mark's

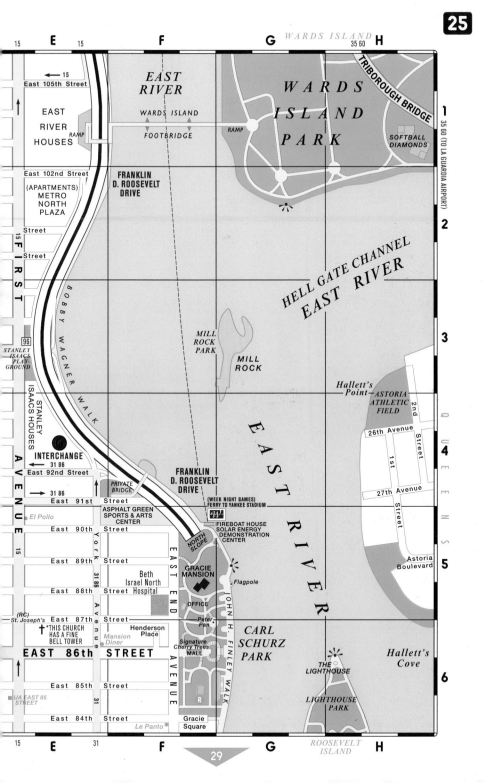

WARDS ISLAND

35 60

15   E   15   F   G   H

35 60 (TO LA GUARDIA AIRPORT)

← 15
East 105th Street

EAST
RIVER

EAST
RIVER
HOUSES

RAMP

EAST
RIVER

WARDS ISLAND
FOOTBRIDGE

RAMP

WARDS
ISLAND
PARK

TRIBOROUGH BRIDGE

SOFTBALL
DIAMONDS

1

East 102nd Street

(APARTMENTS)
METRO
NORTH
PLAZA

FRANKLIN
D. ROOSEVELT
DRIVE

2

Street

15
F
I
R
S
T

Street

HELL GATE CHANNEL
EAST RIVER

96

STANLEY
ISAACS
PLAY-
GROUND

BOBBY WAGNER WALK

MILL
ROCK
PARK

MILL
ROCK

3

Hallett's
Point

ASTORIA
ATHLETIC
FIELD

2nd

Street

STANLEY
ISAACS
HOUSES

E   A   S   T

26th Avenue

1st

Street

Q
U
E
E
N
S

4

A
V
E
N
U
E

INTERCHANGE
31 86

El Pollo

East 92nd Street

→ 31 86

East 91st   Street

PRIVATE
BRIDGE

FRANKLIN
D. ROOSEVELT
DRIVE

(WEEK NIGHT GAMES)
FERRY TO YANKEE STADIUM

27th Avenue

Street

E
A
S
T

R
I
V
E
R

Astoria
Boulevard

15

ASPHALT GREEN
SPORTS & ARTS
CENTER

East 90th   Street

York

East 89th   Street

31 86

Beth
Israel North
Hospital

East 88th   Street

Street

(RC)
St. Joseph's   East 87th   Street

E
N
D

A
V
E
N
U
E

FIREBOAT HOUSE
SOLAR ENERGY
DEMONSTRATION
CENTER

NORTH SLOPE

GRACIE
MANSION

OFFICE

Peter
Pan

Flagpole

J
O
H
N   H.   F
I
N
L
E
Y   W
A
L
K

5

† *THIS CHURCH
HAS A FINE
BELL TOWER

Henderson
Place

Mansion
Diner

EAST   86th   STREET

Signature
Cherry Trees
MALL

CARL
SCHURZ
PARK

Hallett's
Cove

East 85th   Street

UA EAST 85
STREET

31

A
V
E
N
U
E

R

THE
LIGHTHOUSE

LIGHTHOUSE
PARK

6

East 84th   Street

Le Panto

Gracie
Square

15   E   31   F   G   H

29

ROOSEVELT
ISLAND

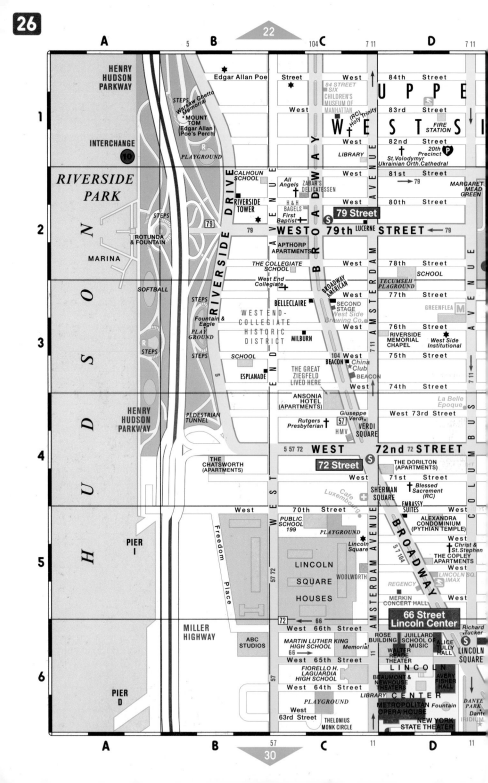

26

A 5 B 104 C 7 11 D 7 11

22

1

HENRY
HUDSON
PARKWAY

Edgar Allan Poe

Street

West 84th Street

STEPS
Warsaw Ghetto
Memorial

84 STREET
SIX
CHILDREN'S
MUSEUM OF
MANHATTAN

U P P E

MOUNT
TOM
(Edgar Allan
Poe's Perch)

West 83rd Street

W + E S T S I

(RC)
Holy Trinity

INTERCHANGE

R

PLAYGROUND

West 82nd Street

LIBRARY

20th
Precinct

FIRE
STATION

St.Volodymyr
Ukrainian Orth.Cathedral

2

*RIVERSIDE
PARK*

H
U
D
S
O
N

CALHOUN
SCHOOL

West 81st Street

→ 79

MARGARET
MEAD
GREEN

RIVERSIDE
TOWER

All Angels

ZABAR'S
DELICATESSEN

West 80th Street

STEPS

H & H
BAGELS
First Baptist

79 Street

ROTUNDA
& FOUNTAIN

79

WEST 79th LUCERNE **STREET** ← 79

MARINA

APTHORP
APARTMENTS

3

SOFTBALL

THE COLLEGIATE
SCHOOL

West 78th Street

SCHOOL

West End
Collegiate

TECUMSEH
PLAYGROUND

Fountain &
Eagle
PLAY
GROUND

STEPS

BELLECLAIRE

WEST END-
COLLEGIATE
HISTORIC
DISTRICT

West 77th Street

SECOND
STAGE
West Side
Brewing Co.

GREENFLEA M

RIVERSIDE
MEMORIAL
CHAPEL

West Side
Institutional

R
STEPS

MILBURN

West 76th Street

SCHOOL

ESPLANADE

STEPS

104 West
BEACON

China
Club
BEACON

West 75th Street

THE GREAT
ZIEGFELD
LIVED HERE

West 74th Street

4

HENRY
HUDSON
PARKWAY

PEDESTRIAN
TUNNEL

ANSONIA
HOTEL
(APARTMENTS)

Rutgers
Presbyterian

Giuseppe
Verdi

57

West 73rd Street

La Belle
Epoque

HMV

VERDI
SQUARE

5 57 72

WEST 72nd STREET

THE
CHATSWORTH
(APARTMENTS)

72 Street

West 71st Street

THE DORILTON
(APARTMENTS)

Café
Luxembourg

SHERMAN
SQUARE

Blessed
Sacrement
(RC)

EMBASSY
SUITES

5

PIER
I

Freedom Place

West 70th Street

PUBLIC
SCHOOL
199

PLAYGROUND

Lincoln
Square

ALEXANDRA
CONDOMINIUM
(PYTHIAN TEMPLE)

Christ &
St. Stephen
THE COPLEY
APARTMENTS

West

LINCOLN
SQUARE
HOUSES

57 72

WOOLWORTH

LINCOLN SQ.
IMAX

REGENCY

West

MERKIN
CONCERT HALL

West

72 ← 66

**66 Street
Lincoln Center**

6

MILLER
HIGHWAY

ABC
STUDIOS

West 66th Street

MARTIN LUTHER
KING
HIGH SCHOOL

66

Memorial

ROSE
BUILDING

JUILLARD
SCHOOL OF
MUSIC

ALICE
TULLY
HALL

Richard
Tucker

LINCOLN
SQUARE

WALTER
READE
THEATER

West 65th Street

FIORELLO H.
LAGUARDIA
HIGH SCHOOL

57

L I N C O L N

PIER
D

West 64th Street

PLAYGROUND

BEAUMONT &
NEWHOUSE
THEATERS

AVERY
FISHER
HALL

LIBRARY **C E N T E R**

West 63rd Street

THELONIUS
MONK CIRCLE

METROPOLITAN
OPERA HOUSE

Fountain

NEW YORK
STATE THEATER

DANTE
PARK

Dante

IRIDIUM

A 57 B C 11 D 11

30

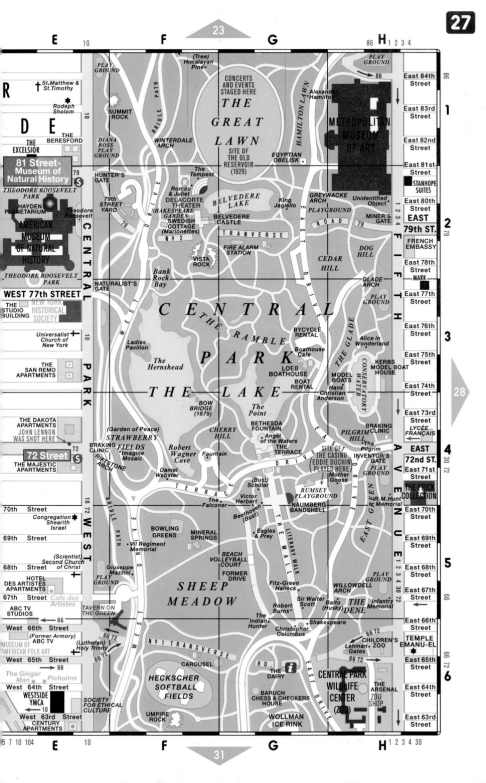

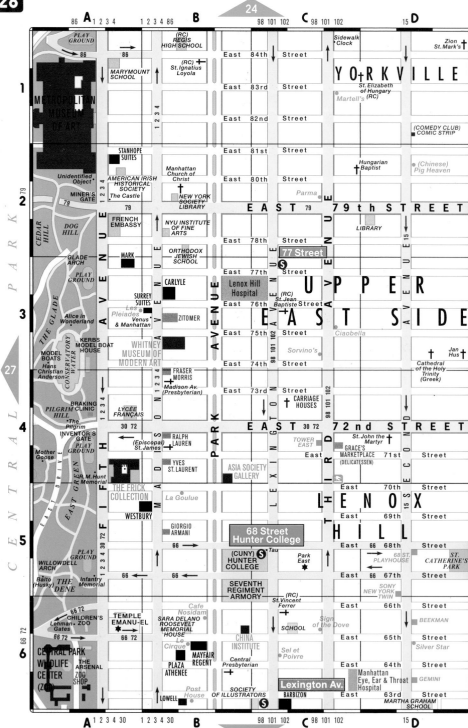

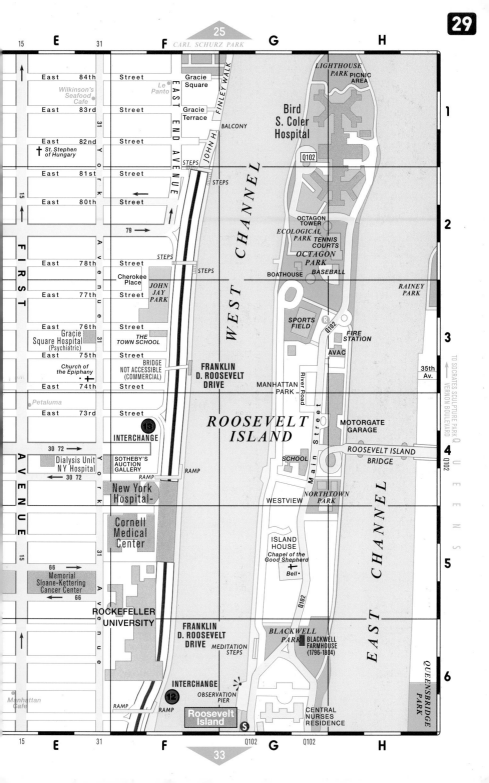

15   E   31   F   G   H

East   84th   Street
Wilkinson's
Seafood
Cafe
Le
Panto
Gracie
Square

LIGHTHOUSE
PARK   PICNIC
AREA

Bird
S. Coler
Hospital

East   83rd   Street
Gracie
Terrace

Q102

East   82nd   Street
† St. Stephen
of Hungary
BALCONY

STEPS

East   81st   Street

STEPS

East   80th   Street

79

OCTAGON
TOWER

ECOLOGICAL
PARK   TENNIS
COURTS

OCTAGON
PARK

East   78th   Street
STEPS

STEPS

BOATHOUSE   BASEBALL

RAINEY
PARK

Cherokee
Place
JOHN
JAY
PARK

East   77th   Street

East   76th   Street
Gracie
Square Hospital
(Psychiatric)
THE
TOWN SCHOOL

SPORTS
FIELD

R

Q102

FIRST

East   75th   Street
Church of
the Epiphany †

BRIDGE
NOT ACCESSIBLE
(COMMERCIAL)

FRANKLIN
D. ROOSEVELT
DRIVE

FIRE
STATION

AVAC

East   74th   Street

MANHATTAN
PARK

River Road

35th
Av.

Petaluma

East   73rd   Street

ROOSEVELT
ISLAND

MOTORGATE
GARAGE

13 INTERCHANGE

30 72

Dialysis Unit
N Y Hospital

SOTHEBY'S
AUCTION
GALLERY

RAMP

RAMP

SCHOOL

Main Street

ROOSEVELT ISLAND
BRIDGE

Q102

30 72

New York
Hospital-

WESTVIEW

NORTHTOWN
PARK

AVENUE

Cornell
Medical
Center

ISLAND
HOUSE
Chapel of the
Good Shepherd
Bell •

66

Memorial
Sloane-Kettering
Cancer Center
66

ROCKEFELLER
UNIVERSITY

FRANKLIN
D. ROOSEVELT
DRIVE
MEDITATION
STEPS

BLACKWELL
PARK   BLACKWELL
FARMHOUSE
(1796-1804)

EAST   CHANNEL

WEST   CHANNEL

ROOSEVELT
ISLAND

INTERCHANGE

12

RAMP

RAMP

OBSERVATION
PIER

Roosevelt
Island

S

CENTRAL
NURSES
RESIDENCE

QUEENSBRIDGE
PARK

Manhattan
Cafe

15   E   31   F   G   H

Q102   Q102

TO SOCRATES SCULPTURE PARK
VERNON BOULEVARD

QUEENS

1
2
3
4
5
6

JOHN H. FINLEY WALK
EAST END AVENUE
YORK   AVENUE

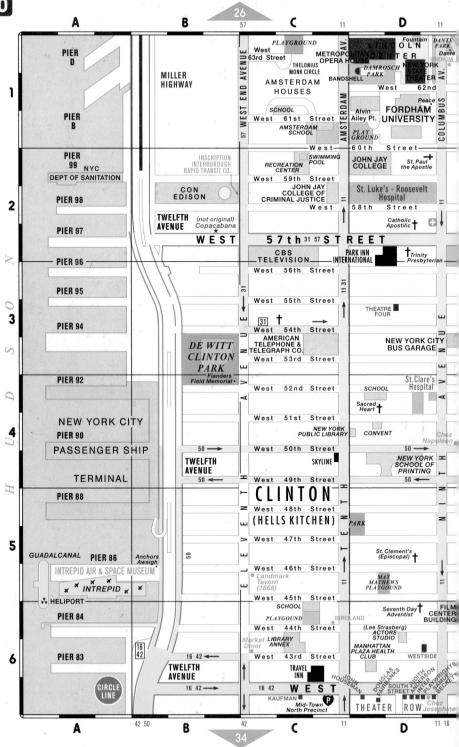

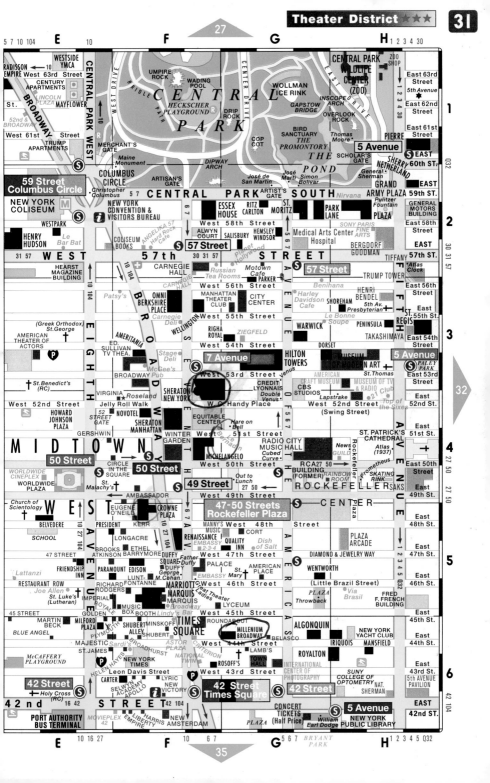

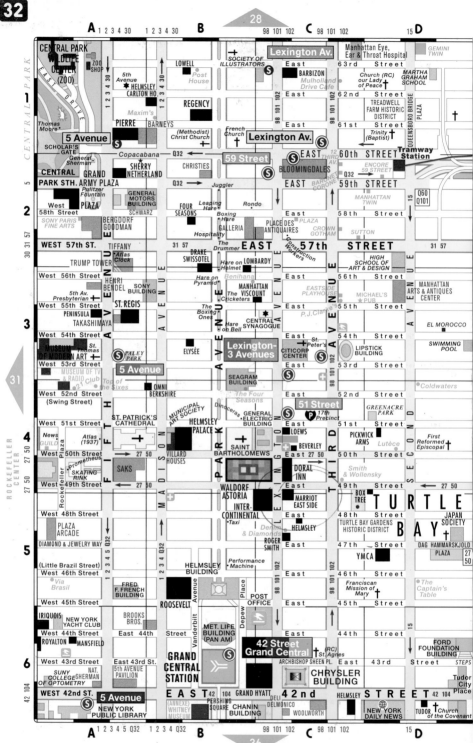

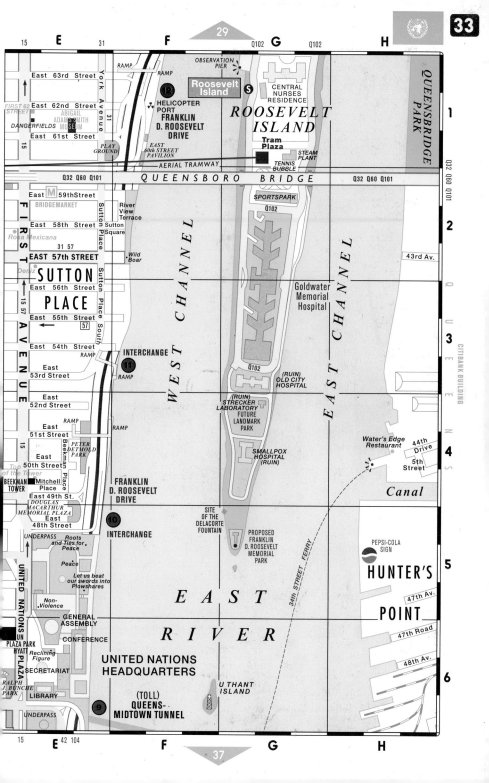

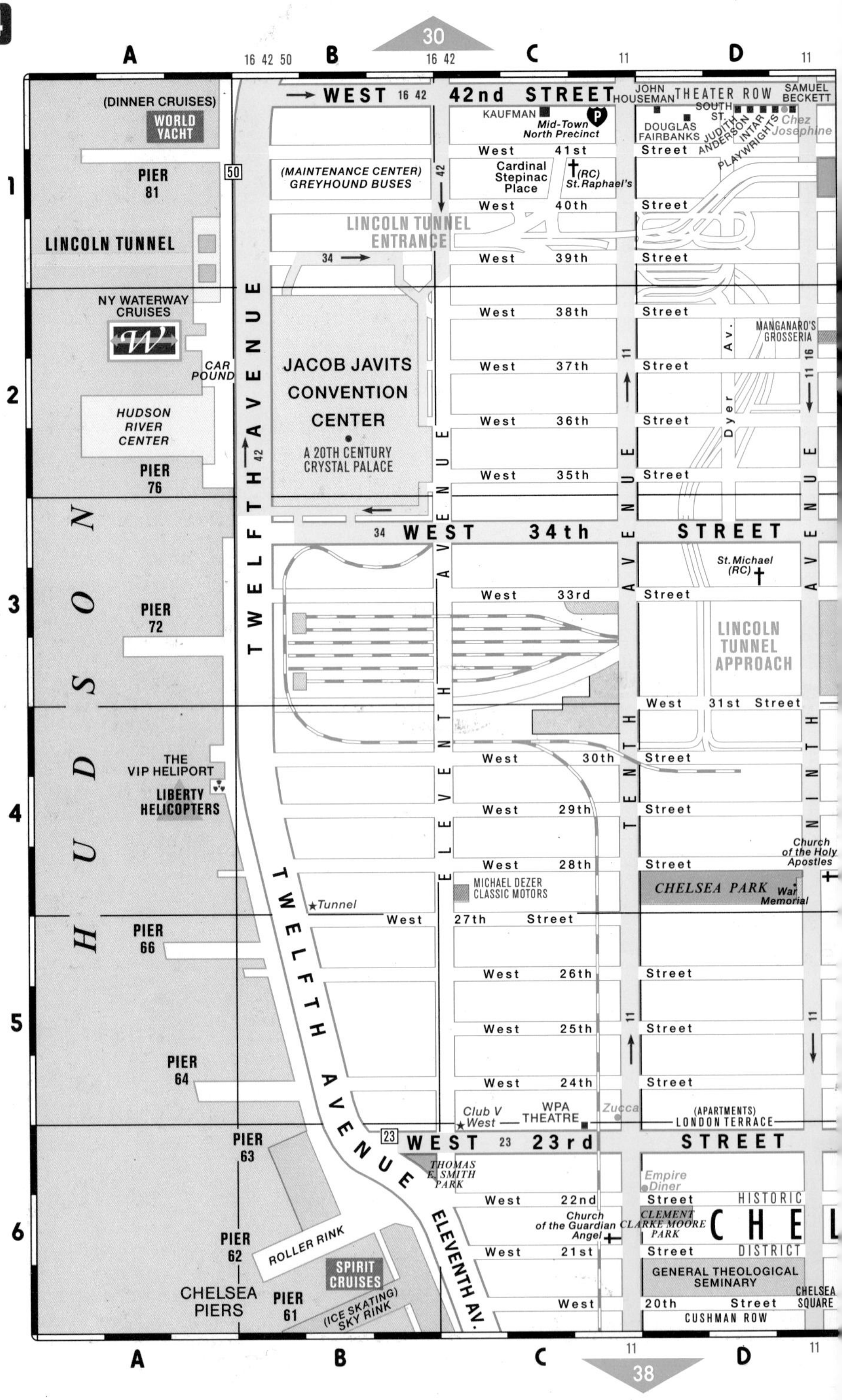

A   16 42 50   B   16 42   C   11   D   11

WEST 16 42 **42nd STREET**

JOHN HOUSEMAN THEATER ROW SAMUEL BECKETT

KAUFMAN P Mid-Town SOUTH ST.

Mid-Town North Precinct

DOUGLAS FAIRBANKS JUDITH ANDERSON INTAR PLAYWRIGHTS Chez Josephine

(DINNER CRUISES)

WORLD YACHT

1

PIER 81

West   41st   Street

Cardinal Stepinac Place

(RC) St. Raphael's

(MAINTENANCE CENTER) GREYHOUND BUSES

LINCOLN TUNNEL

West   40th   Street

50

42

34

LINCOLN TUNNEL ENTRANCE

West   39th   Street

NY WATERWAY CRUISES

W

CAR POUND

JACOB JAVITS CONVENTION CENTER

West   38th   Street

MANGANARO'S GROSSERIA

Av.

11 16

West   37th   Street

2

HUDSON RIVER CENTER

• A 20TH CENTURY CRYSTAL PALACE

West   36th   Street

Dyer

11

PIER 76

West   35th   Street

T W E L F T H   A V E N U E

42

34

WEST   34th   STREET

St. Michael (RC) ✝

H U D S O N

PIER 72

West   33rd   Street

LINCOLN TUNNEL APPROACH

3

West   31st Street

THE VIP HELIPORT

West   30th   Street

LIBERTY HELICOPTERS

West   29th   Street

T E N T H   A V E N U E

N I N T H   A V E N U E

4

West   28th   Street

Church of the Holy Apostles ✝

★Tunnel

MICHAEL DEZER CLASSIC MOTORS

CHELSEA PARK War Memorial

PIER 66

West   27th   Street

E L E V E N T H

West   26th   Street

5

PIER 64

West   25th   Street

11

11

West   24th   Street

Club V ★ West

WPA THEATRE

Zucca

(APARTMENTS) LONDON TERRACE

PIER 63

23 **WEST** 23 **23rd   STREET**

THOMAS F. SMITH PARK

Empire • Diner

HISTORIC

T W E L F T H   A V E N U E

West   22nd   Street

C H E L

Church of the Guardian Angel ✝

CLEMENT CLARKE MOORE PARK

6

PIER 62

ROLLER RINK

West   21st   Street

DISTRICT

SPIRIT CRUISES

GENERAL THEOLOGICAL SEMINARY

CHELSEA SQUARE

CHELSEA PIERS

PIER 61

(ICE SKATING) SKY RINK

E L E V E N T H AV.

West   20th   Street

CUSHMAN ROW

A   B   C   11   D   11

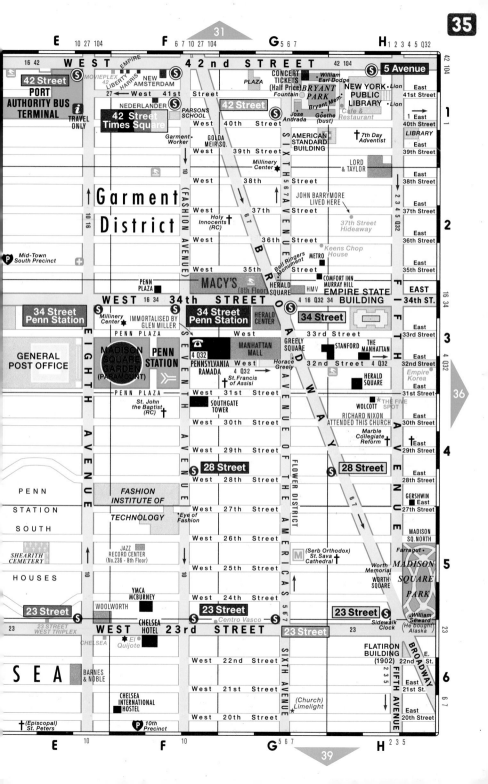

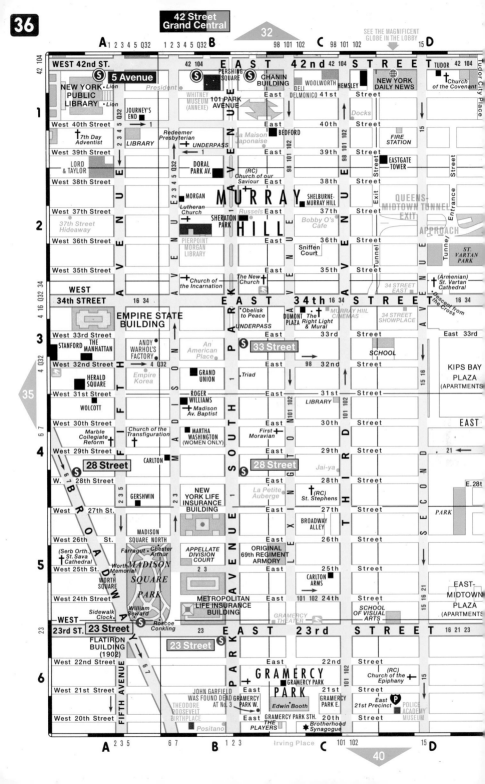

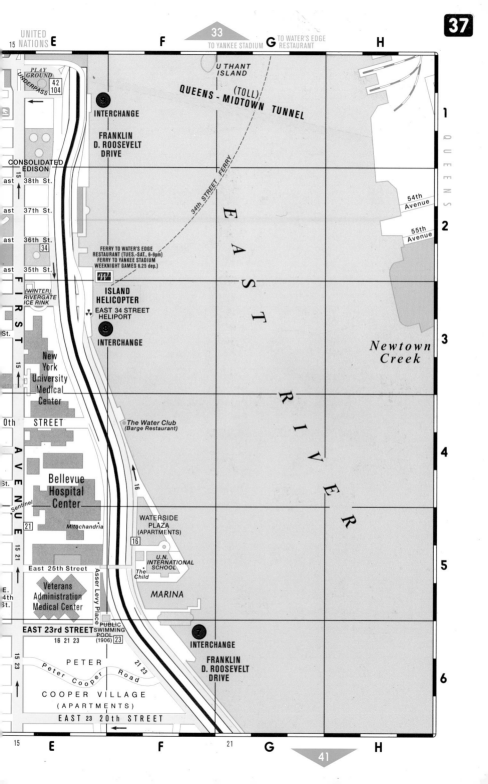

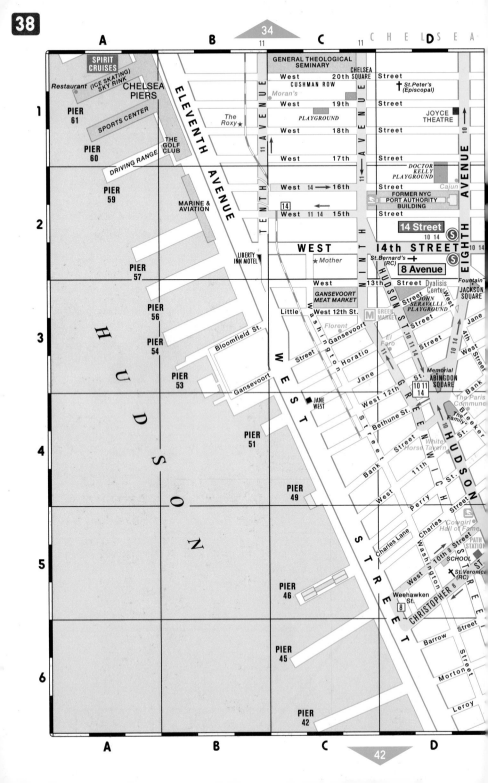

CHELSEA

34

42

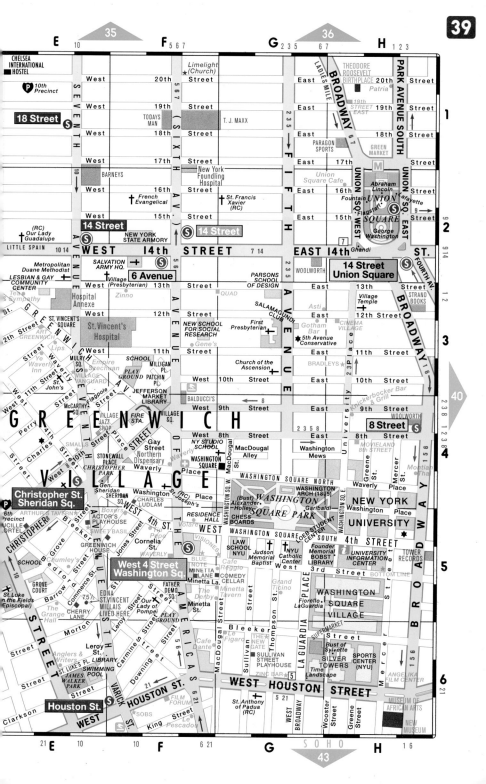

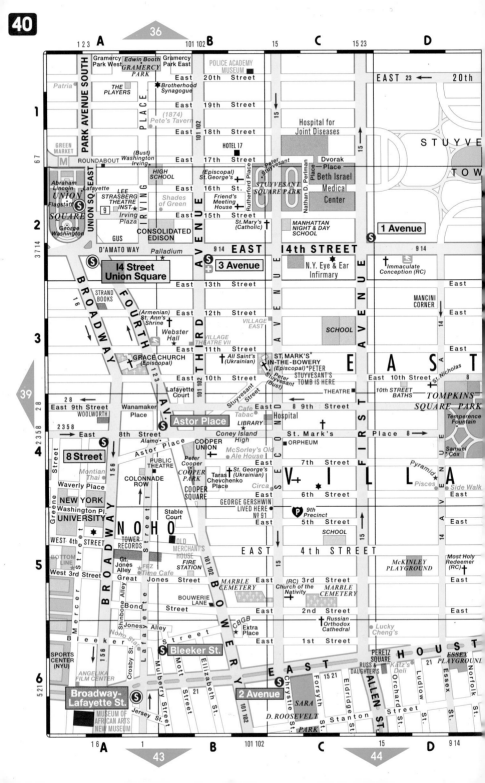

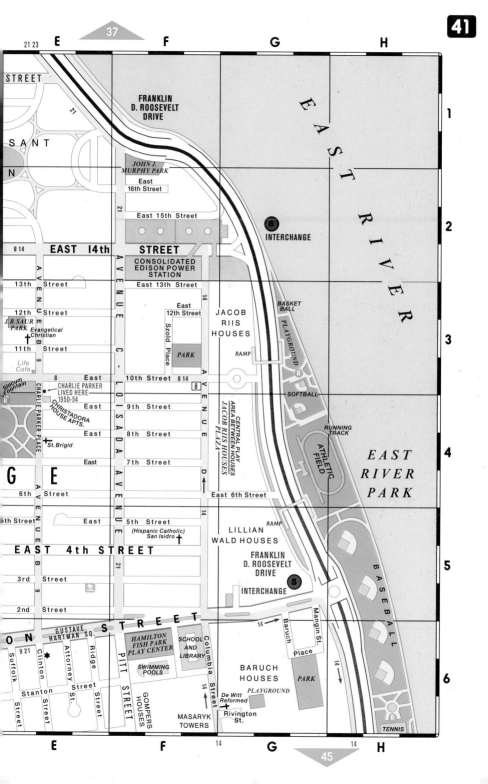

STREET

FRANKLIN
D. ROOSEVELT
DRIVE

1

SANT

N

JOHN J.
MURPHY PARK

East
16th Street

East 15th Street

E A S T   R I V E R

2

9 14

EAST 14th   STREET

6
INTERCHANGE

CONSOLIDATED
EDISON POWER
STATION

East 13th Street

13th   Street

East
12th Street

JACOB

BASKET
BALL

12th   Street

J.B. SAUR
PARK

Evangelical
Christian

Szold Place

East

RIIS

3

HOUSES

PARK

11th   Street

RAMP

Life
Cafe

East   10th Street   8 14

8

Slocum
Fountain

8

East

CHARLIE PARKER
LIVED HERE
1950-54

9th   Street

SOFTBALL

RAMP

CHARLIE PARKER PLACE

CHRISTADORA
HOUSE APTS.

East

8th   Street

CENTRAL PLAY
AREA BETWEEN HOUSES
JACOB RIIS HOUSES
PLAZA

ATHLETIC
FIELD

RUNNING
TRACK

PLAYGROUND

St. Brigid

East

7th   Street

4

G

E

AVENUE C · LOISADA AVENUE

AVENUE D

East

EAST
RIVER
PARK

6th   Street

East 6th Street

6th Street

East

5th   Street

LILLIAN
WALD HOUSES

(Hispanic Catholic)
San Isidro

RAMP

EAST   4th   STREET

FRANKLIN
D. ROOSEVELT
DRIVE

3rd   Street

5
INTERCHANGE

5

B A S E B A L L

2nd   Street

Mangin St.

Baruch

ON   STREET

GUSTAVE
HARTMAN SQ.

14

Place

9 21

Clinton

Attorney

Ridge

PITT

HAMILTON
FISH PARK
PLAY CENTER

SCHOOL
AND
LIBRARY

Columbia

BARUCH

Street

Suffolk

Street

St.

SWIMMING
POOLS

STREET

Street

HOUSES

PARK

6

Stanton

Street

Street

Street

GOMPERS
HOUSES

PLAYGROUND

De Witt
Reformed

R

Street

14

MASARYK
TOWERS

Rivington
St.

TENNIS

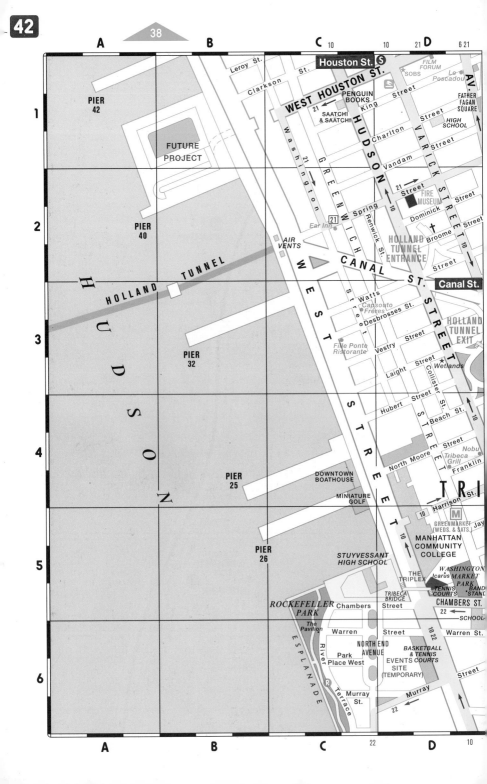

38

A   B   C 10   10   21 D   6 21

Leroy St.
Clarkson   St.   Houston St. (S)
WEST HOUSTON ST.

1
PIER 42
FUTURE PROJECT

PENGUIN BOOKS
SAATCHI & SAATCHI
21   King   Street
Charlton   Street
Washington   21   Vandam

FILM FORUM
SOBS
Le Pescadou
FATHER FAGAN SQUARE
HIGH SCHOOL

HUDSON   St
Greenwich   Street
VARICK STREET AV.

2
PIER 40

AIR VENTS

Street   21   Street
Spring   10
FIRE MUSEUM
Dominick
Broome   Street   Street

Ear Inn   21
Renwick   St.
CANAL   ST.

HOLLAND   TUNNEL
HUDSON

HOLLAND TUNNEL ENTRANCE
Street
Canal St.

WEST

Watts
Capsouto Frères
Desbrosses   St.

HOLLAND TUNNEL EXIT

3
PIER 32

Fille Ponte Ristorante
Vestry   Street

Wetlands
Laight   Street
Collister St.

ST.
Hubert   Street   St.
Beach St.

4
PIER 25

STREET

North Moore   Street
Nobu
Tribeca Grill   Franklin
Harrison   St.

DOWNTOWN BOATHOUSE
MINIATURE GOLF

T R I
10
10   Harrison
M
GREENMARKET (WEDS. & SATS.)   Jay

5
PIER 26

STUYVESSANT HIGH SCHOOL

MANHATTAN COMMUNITY COLLEGE

WASHINGTON MARKET PARK
Icarus   BAND STAND
THE TRIPLEX
TENNIS COURTS
TRIBECA BRIDGE
CHAMBERS ST.

ROCKEFELLER PARK   Chambers   Street
22   SCHOOL

6
ESPLANADE

The Pavilion
Warren   Street   Warren St.
NORTH END AVENUE
Park Place West
River Terrace   Murray St.

BASKETBALL & TENNIS COURTS
EVENTS SITE (TEMPORARY)
10 22   Street

R
Murray   22

A   B   C   22   D   10

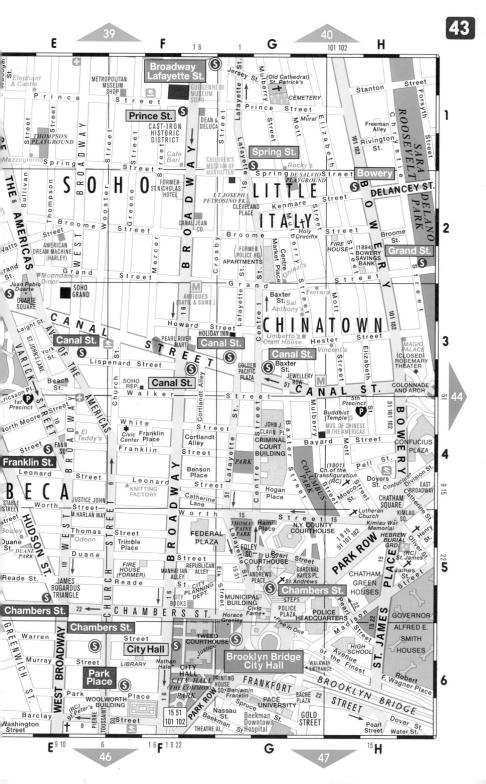

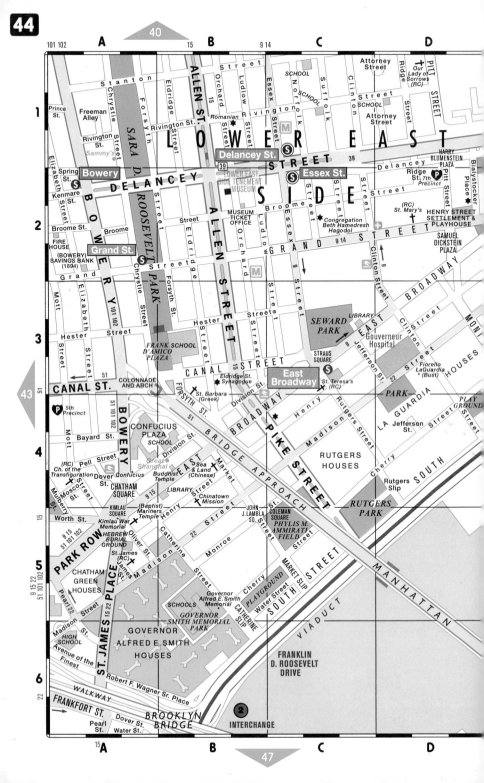

101 102   A   40   15   B   9 14   C   D

LOWER EAST STREET

SIDE

Prince St.
Freeman Alley
Stanton Street
Orchard Street
Ludlow Street
Essex Street
Norfolk Street
SCHOOL
Suffolk Street
Clinton Street
Attorney Street
Ridge Street
Our Lady of Sorrows (RC)
PITT STREET

Chrystie
Forsyth
Eldridge Street
Rivington St.
Romanian Rivington Street
SCHOOL
Attorney Street
SCHOOL

1

Rivington St.
Elizabeth
Sammy's
SARA
DELANCEY Street
Delancey St.
Delancey Street
HARRY BLUMENSTEIN PLAZA
Blalystocker Place

Spring St.
Bowery
Kenmare St.
Romanian
LOWER EAST SIDE TENEMENT MUSEUM
Essex St.
Ridge St. 7th Precinct

ROOSEVELT

Broome St.
FIRE HOUSE
(BOWERY SAVINGS BANK (1894)
Grand St.
Broome
MUSEUM TICKET OFFICE
Eldridge Street
Orchard Street
Ludlow Street
Broome
Essex Street
GRAND
Congregation Beth Hamedresh Hagodol
(RC) St. Mary's
HENRY STREET SETTLEMENT & PLAYHOUSE
SAMUEL DICKSTEIN PLAZA

2

B O W E R Y
Chrystie
PARK
Forsyth Street
Street
STREET
Clinton Street
BROADWAY
MONT

Grand

Mott
Elizabeth
101 102
Hester Street
Street
FRANK D'AMICO PLAZA
SCHOOL PLAZA
Hester Street
Street
Street
SEWARD PARK
LIBRARY
EAST
Gouverneur Hospital
Jefferson Street
Fiorello LaGuardia* (Bust)
HOUSES

3

43   51   CANAL ST.   51   CANAL STREET
STRAUS SQUARE
East Broadway
St. Teresa's (RC)
PARK
PLAY GROUND

COLONNADE AND ARCH
Eldridge St. Synagogue
St. Barbara (Greek)
Division St.
BROADWAY
EAST BROADWAY
Henry Street
Rutgers Street
Madison Street
LA GUARDIA
Jefferson St.
Cherry Street
SOUTH

5th Precinct
51 101 102
CONFUCIUS PLAZA
SCHOOL
FORSYTH ST.
BRIDGE APPROACH
PIKE STREET
RUTGERS HOUSES
Rutgers Slip

4

Mott
Bayard St.
(RC) Ch. of the Transfiguration
Pell Street
Dover St.
Great Shanghai
Confucius
Sea & Land (Chinese)
Buddhist Temple
Market Street
RUTGERS PARK

Mulberry
Moscow St.
CHATHAM SQUARE
LIBRARY
Chinatown Mission
JOHN J.LAMBLA SQ.
St.
COLEMAN SQUARE
PHYLIS M. AMMIRATI FIELD

Worth St.
KIMLAU SQUARE
(Baptist) Mariners Temple
Henry
22
Monroe
Street
MANHATTAN

5

15
9 15
51 101 102
PARK ROW
Kimlau War Memorial
HEBREW BURIAL GROUND
St. James (RC)
Oliver St.
Catherine Street
22
Street
PLAYGROUND
Cherry Street
Water Street
Market Slip
SOUTH STREET

Pearl 22
CHATHAM GREEN HOUSES
ST. JAMES PLACE
15 22
James St.
Madison Street
Governor Alfred E. Smith Memorial
CATHERINE SLIP
VIADUCT

Madison
HIGH SCHOOL
Avenue of the Finest
GOVERNOR SMITH MEMORIAL PARK
SCHOOLS
GOVERNOR ALFRED E. SMITH HOUSES
FRANKLIN D. ROOSEVELT DRIVE

6

22   WALKWAY
FRANKFORT ST.
Robert F. Wagner Sr. Place
Pearl St.
Dover St.
Water St.
BROOKLYN BRIDGE
2
INTERCHANGE

15   A   B   47   C   D

E 14   **F** 14   **G**   **H**

39

De Witt
Reformed

Rivington
St.

PARK

Columbia
Street

14

DELANCEY STREET

1

BRIDGE APPROACH

South

RAMP

WILLIAMSBURG BRIDGE

39

TENNIS

R

Street

Cannon
St.

Broome
St.

Columbia
Street

ABRAHAM E.
KAZAN STREET

Lewis
Street

**FRANKLIN
D. ROOSEVELT
DRIVE**

PLAY
AREA

FIRE
HOUSE

BERNARD
DOWNING
PLAYGROUND

GRAND

RHEDA
LIEBOWITZ
SQ.

AHERN
PARK

St.
Augustine's
Episcopal

RITUAL
BATH
HOUSE

HENRY St.
M. JACKSON
PLAYGROUND

Henry   Street

Madison   Street

SAMUEL
A.SPIEGEL
SQ.

ST.

14

Jackson

14
22

14
22

St. 22   SQ.

INTERCHANGE

*EAST
RIVER
PARK*

SOFTBALL
FIELD

2

VLADECK PARK

22

14 22

Cherry

Flagpole

Jackson   Street

Street

RAMP

*CORLEAR'S
HOOK
PARK
PLAYGROUND*

OPEN AIR
THEATRE
(DERELICT)

**CORLEAR'S
HOOK**

FIRE
HOUSE

L.D.WALD
PLAYGROUND

Gouverneur   Street

ST. ROSE'S
HOME

Water
Street

EAST
GOUVERNEUR
SLIP

East   Street

3

GOMERY ST.

Front   Street

WEST

Marginal   Street

STREET

EAST   RIVER

4

*Wallabout
Bay*

CONSOLIDATED EDISON
HUDSON RIVER STATION

Marshall St.

Gold   Street

Hudson   Avenue

Little
St.

Evans Street

FORMER NAVAL
COMMANDANTS
HOUSE

HARRISON
ALLEY

BROOKLYN

NAVY YARD

5

VINEGAR

HILL

John   Street

Jay   Street

Bridge   Street

Plymouth Street

Water   Street

(RC)
St.Ann's

St.
George's

Navy   Street

INDUSTRIAL

PARK

BRIDGE

Adams
St.

Pearl   Street

Anchorage
Pl.

Front   Street

York   Street

Street

Street

6

East
Washington
St.

E   **F**   **G**   **H**

51

48

BROOKLYN

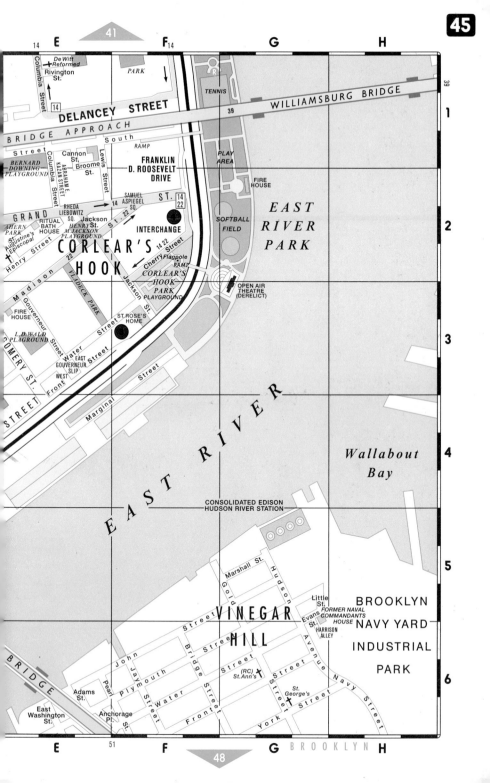

42

ESPLANADE

River Terrace

Vesey

Murray St.

LILY POOL Place

North End Avenue

(NYNEX) N.Y. TELEPHONE CO. BUILDING

GREENWICH ST.

Barclay

Washington St.

WOOLWORTH BUILDING

9 Pierre TOUSSAINT SQ.

St. Peter's (RC)

Street

J & R MUSIC WORLD

PARK ROW

Beekman St.

St.

15 51 101 102

22 →

VESEY STREET

22 4

R

MERRILL LYNCH

AMERICAN EXPRESS

3

WEST BROADWAY

VESEY ST. 1 9 22

Three Red Wings

THEATRE ALLEY

Ann St.

Nassau

HOBOKEN FERRY

WORLD

FINANCIAL

WINTER GARDEN

NORTH BRIDGE

9 10 22

6

U.S. CUSTOM HOUSE

S

ST. PAUL'S CHAPEL

FULTON ST.

Dutch St.

Broadway Nassau St.

FUL

1

North Cove

NORTH TOWER

1

World Trade Center

5

MILLENIUM

Dey St.

John

WHITNEY DOWNTOWN MUSEUM

BATTERY PARK CITY

YACHT HARBOUR

Police Memorial

CENTER

MERRILL LYNCH

NORTH GATEHOUSE

Ideogram*

SOUTH TOWER (OBSERVATORY)

Fountain & Sphere*

4

Sculpture

Cortlandt St.

CENTURY 21

S

Cortland St.

Maiden

Liberty Place

FEDERAL RESERVE BANK

John St. United Methodist

WHITNEY DOWNTOWN MUSEUM

Lane

GATEWAY PLAZA

SOUTH GATEHOUSE

DOW JONES

Liberty St.

VISTA HOTEL

3

Cortlandt St.

Double Check

LIBERTY PARK

Red Cube

Liberty

Street

CHASE MANHATTAN PLAZA

EQUITABLE BUILDING

2

Esplanade

HUDSON

South

End

Street

9 10

Albany

MARRIOTT

TUNNEL ENTRANCE

SOUTH BRIDGE

Cedar St.

Cedardag

Washington St.

Greenwich St.

Thames

Street

Albany St.

Carlisle St.

(Episcopal) TRINITY CHURCH

Cedar St.

Pine

TRINITY PLACE

AMERICAN STOCK EXCHANGE

MORGAN BANK

Sunken Garden

FEDERAL HALL

S

The Upper Room

Albany Street

RECTOR PARK

Rector Place

West Place

Rector St.

Rector St.

S

Rector Street

John Watts

S

Rector St.

Edgar St.

U.S. STOCK EXCHANGE

George

Washington

New St.

Wall St.

S

Wall St.

FINAN

WEST THAMES PARK

West Thames St.

Exchange Alley

Exchange

Place

WALL

BROAD STREET

3

Third Pl.

Brooklyn Battery Tunnel

6

Morris St.

Morris St.

Broad St.

ORIGINAL STANDARD OIL BUILDING

DIST

South St.

William St.

South Cove

BRIDGE

South Place

Second Place

DOWNTOWN ATHLETIC CLUB

Battery Place

Greenwich St.

Charging Bull

BOWLING GREEN PARK

Beaver St.

Marketfield Street

Whitehall St.

Stone St.

HOLOCAUST MEMORIAL

First Place

TUNNEL TO FDR DRIVE

Washington St.

Bowling Green

S

NATIONAL MUSEUM OF THE AMERICAN INDIAN U.S. CUSTOM HOUSE

FRAUNCES TAVERN

4

MUSEUM OF JEWISH HERITAGE

ROBERT F. WAGNER JR. PARK

Bugle & Mandolin

Jerusalem Grove

Flagpole

Walloon Settler

Netherland Memorial

STATE STREET

Moore St.

Pearl St.

17 STATE

15

BATTERY PLACE

John Ericsson

Fort George Memorial

The Immigrants

Bridge

SHRINE OF ELIZABETH SETON

PIER A

American Merchant Mariners Memorial

CASTLE CLINTON

BATTERY PARK

PETER MINUIT PLAZA

Emma Lazarus Memorial

FERRY LANDING

Giovanni da Verrazano

Wireless Operators Mem.

Cannon

South Ferry

R

5

STATUE OF LIBERTY ELLIS ISLAND FERRY

ADMIRAL DEWEY PROMENADE

Norwegian Mem.

East Coast War Mem.

Coast Guard Memorial

1 6 15

S

John Wolf Ambrose (Bust)

COASTGUARD BUILDING

COLGATE CLOCK

ELLIS ISLAND

STATUE OF LIBERTY — ELLIS ISLAND

BROOKLYN BATTERY TUNNEL

6

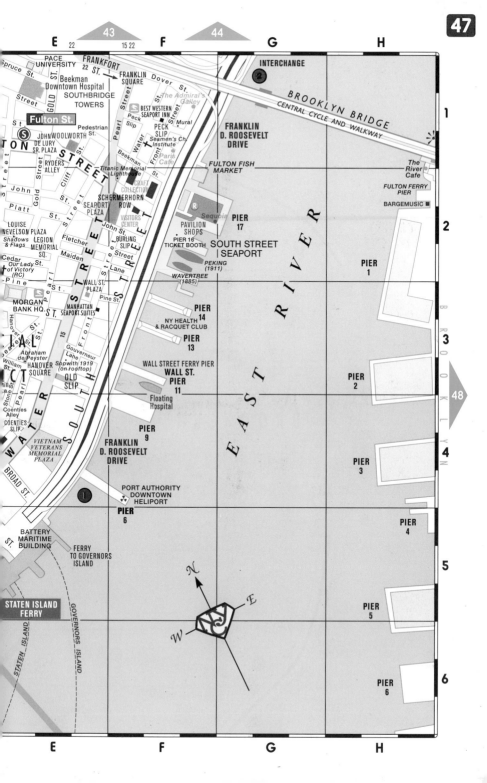

PACE UNIVERSITY
Spruce St.
FRANKFORT ST.
22
Beekman Downtown Hospital
SOUTHBRIDGE TOWERS

Fulton St.
Ⓢ

Franklin SQUARE

Dover St.
The Admiral's Galley

INTERCHANGE ②

BROOKLYN BRIDGE
CENTRAL CYCLE AND WALKWAY

JOHN WOOLWORTH DE LURY SR. PLAZA
RYDERS ALLEY
Pedestrian St.

BEST WESTERN SEAPORT INN
Peck Slip
Water
Front St.

PECK SLIP
Mural
Seamen's Ch. Institute
Paris Cafe

FRANKLIN D. ROOSEVELT DRIVE

The River Cafe

FULTON FERRY PIER
BARGEMUSIC ■

Beekman St.
Titanic Memorial Lighthouse
CRAFT COLLECTION

FULTON FISH MARKET

John St.
Platt St.
SEAPORT PLAZA
SCHERMERHORN ROW
VISITORS CENTER
BURLING SLIP

LOUISE NEVELSON PLAZA
Shadows & Flags
LEGION MEMORIAL SQ.
Fletcher St.
John St.
Fletcher St.
Maiden Lane

R
Sequoia

PIER 17

PIER 16 TICKET BOOTH
PAVILION SHOPS
SOUTH STREET SEAPORT
PEKING (1911)

Cedar
Our Lady of Victory (RC)
-Pine
Pine St.
WALL ST. PLAZA

WAVERTREE (1885)

EAST RIVER

PIER 2

MORGAN BANK HQ.
MANHATTAN SEAPORT SUITES
Pine St.

PIER 14
NY HEALTH & RACQUET CLUB

IAL
15
Abraham de Peyster
HANOVER SQUARE
Gouverneur Lane
Sopwith 1919 (on rooftop)
OLD SLIP

PIER 13

CT
William St.
Stone
Coenties Alley
COENTIES SLIP

WALL STREET FERRY PIER
WALL ST. PIER 11
Floating Hospital

PIER 2

PIER 9

WATER
VIETNAM VETERANS MEMORIAL PLAZA
FRANKLIN D. ROOSEVELT DRIVE

PIER 3

BROAD ST.
ⓘ
PORT AUTHORITY DOWNTOWN HELIPORT

PIER 6

PIER 4

BATTERY MARITIME BUILDING
ST.
FERRY TO GOVERNORS ISLAND

STATEN ISLAND FERRY
STATEN ISLAND
GOVERNORS ISLAND

N
E
W
S

PIER 5

PIER 6

BROOKLYN ▶ 48

1

2

3

4

5

6

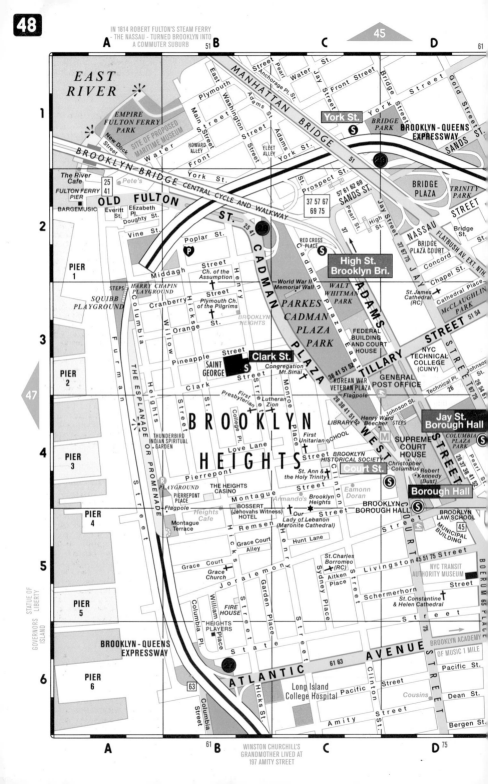

IN 1814 ROBERT FULTON'S STEAM FERRY
THE NASSAU – TURNED BROOKLYN INTO
A COMMUTER SUBURB

EAST RIVER

EMPIRE FULTON FERRY PARK

SITE OF PROPOSED MARITIME MUSEUM

New Dock Street

Water Street

BROOKLYN BRIDGE

The River Cafe

FULTON FERRY PIER

BARGEMUSIC

25 41

Pete's

OLD FULTON ST.

Everitt St.

Elizabeth Pl.

Doughty St.

Vine St.

Poplar St.

Middagh Street

HARRY CHAPIN PLAYGROUND

Cranberry Street

SQUIBB PLAYGROUND

Columbia Heights

Willow

Hicks

Orange Street

Pineapple Street

SAINT GEORGE

Clark Street

Clark St.

Congregation Mt. Sinai

First Presbyterian

Lutheran Zion

Monroe

BROOKLYN HEIGHTS

Love Lane

First Unitarian

Pierrepont Street

BROOKLYN HISTORICAL SOCIETY

St. Ann & the Holy Trinity

THE HEIGHTS CASINO

PIERREPONT PLACE

PLAYGROUND

Flagpole

Montague Street

Heights Cafe

Montague Terrace

Armando's

Brooklyn Heights

BOSSERT (Jehovahs Witness) HOTEL

Our Lady of Lebanon (Maronite Cathedral)

Remsen Street

Eamonn Doran

Court St.

Brooklyn BOROUGH HALL

Grace Court Alley

Grace Church

Hunt Lane

St. Charles Borromeo (RC)

Joralemon Street

FIRE HOUSE

HEIGHTS PLAYERS

Garden Place

William

State Street

Sidney Place

Aitken Place

Livingston 45 51 75 Street

Schermerhorn Street

St. Constantine & Helen Cathedral

BROOKLYN – QUEENS EXPRESSWAY

63

Columbia Street

ATLANTIC

Hicks St.

Clinton Street

Long Island College Hospital

Pacific

Cousins

Amity Street

AVENUE

61 63

BROOKLYN ACADEMY OF MUSIC 1 MILE

Pacific St.

Dean St.

Bergen St.

MANHATTAN BRIDGE

East Street

Plymouth Street

Main Street

Water Street

Washington Street

Adams Street

Fleet Alley

Howard Alley

Front Street

York St.

Jay Street

Front Street

Pearl Street

Anchorage Pl. St.

Water Street

York St.

BRIDGE PARK

BROOKLYN – QUEENS EXPRESSWAY

York Street

Bridge Street

Gold Street

Sands Street

High St. Brooklyn Bri.

Prospect St.

37 57 67 69 75

57 61 62 66

Sands St.

RED CROSS PLACE

CADMAN

ADAMS

PLAZA

World War II Memorial Wall

PARKES CADMAN PLAZA PARK

WALT WHITMAN PARK

FEDERAL BUILDING AND COURT HOUSE

KOREAN WAR VETERAN PLAZA

Flagpole

38 41 51 52

26 38 41 51

TILLARY STREET

JAY STREET

BRIDGE PLAZA

TRINITY PARK

Bridge St.

NASSAU

FLATBUSH AV. EXT. NTH

BRIDGE PLAZA COURT

Concord

Chapel St.

St. James Cathedral (RC)

Cathedral Place

McCLAUGHLIN PARK

51 54

NYC TECHNICAL COLLEGE (CUNY)

Technical Pl. 26

GENERAL POST OFFICE

LIBRARY SCHOOL

Henry Ward Beecher STEPS

Jay St. Borough Hall

COLUMBIA PLAZA PARK

SUPREME COURT HOUSE

Christopher Columbus

Robert F. Kennedy (Bust)

Borough Hall

BROOKLYN LAW SCHOOL

MUNICIPAL BUILDING

45

NYC TRANSIT AUTHORITY MUSEUM

BOERUM PLACE

65

STATUE OF LIBERTY

GOVERNORS ISLAND

PIER 1

PIER 2

PIER 3

PIER 4

PIER 5

PIER 6

STEPS

THE ESPLANADE OR PROMENADE

Furman Street

THUNDERBIRD INDIAN SPIRITUAL GARDEN

25 41

Ch. of the Assumption

Plymouth Ch. of the Pilgrims

BROOKLYN HEIGHTS

51

61

WINSTON CHURCHILL'S GRANDMOTHER LIVED AT 197 AMITY STREET

75

PARKS AND GARDENS - BEACHES

BATTERY PARK   C5 46
A small park at Manhattan's southern edge filled
with memorials and lively squirrels. You can watch
the ferries from the esplanade, ploughing to and fro
from the distant Statue of Liberty and Ellis Island.

BRYANT PARK   G1 35
A small but lovely mid-Manhattan oasis, with a cafe
and restaurant that overlooks the park at the rear of
the N.Y. Public Library. On one side is the chute-
like Grace Building, next door to the remodelled
SUNY college which was originally Aeolian Hall
where George Gershwin premiered *Rhapsody in Blue*
in 1924. A Crystal Palace - a mirror of London's -
stood on this site until 1858, when it burned down.
*On Monday evenings in summer there are open air film
shows beginning at sundown, but get there by 6pm.*

CARL SCHURZ PARK   G6 25
A compact, well-kept park - the mayor's official
residence, Gracie Mansion, is here. From the
waterfront terrace there are fine panoramic views of
the East River and Hell's Gate, and in a small alcove
there is a statue of Peter Pan rescued from the
Paramount theatre on Broadway.

CENTRAL PARK   Pages 21-23-27-31
Opened in 1859 and located between 59th and 110th
Streets, to my mind this must be the greatest urban
park in the world - it seems to have everything you
could wish for in a park. There is no doubt that the
designers were influenced by the romantic and
heroic landscape paintings of Claude Lorrain. It
certainly is the largest park in any great city, being
2.5 miles long and 840 acres with: woods, lakes,
meadows, bridle paths, playgrounds, gardens, a zoo,
skating rinks, a swimming pool, numerous diverse
sporting facilities and the Metropolitan Museum. It
is so well designed that the traffic roads bisecting
the park are all sunken out of sight: marvelous
foresight by the park's designers - Calvert Vaux and
Frederick Law Olmsted. Nothing seems to intrude
on the landscape. To think such a park is in a city
like New York is amazing and it is so accessible.
A walk along the statue-lined Mall (G5 27) will lead
you to the Bethesda Fountain and Terrace where
across the lake is the wooded maze-like Ramble -
not a place to explore at dusk - but in daytime a
lovely place full of birds and unusual trees and
shrubs. In the appropriately named Strawberry
Fields you will come across an unpretentious Italian
mosaic - usually strewn with flowers - donated by
John Lennon's widow (Yoko Ono) and called
Imagine (F4 27): Lennon was killed across the road
at the side of the Dakota apartments where he lived.
The high point of the park is Vista Rock (F2 27)
which is crowned by the Victorian Gothic-styled
Belvedere Castle; built in 1871, it was once a
weather station. Today it is used as a learning
center. Underneath the castle the transverse road
burrows through the rock. At Grand Army Plaza
(H2 31) there are hansom cabs - horse and carriages
- that will take you for a leisurely clip-clop around
the park in style; you can negotiate fares and tips!
During summer months there are concerts on the
Great Lawn and if you get to the Delacorte open-
air theater (F2 27) early enough, Shakespeare for
free! An easy cycle ride around the park is a good
way to get to know it. Bikes can be hired near the
Loeb Boathouse (G3 27): this is also the place to
hire rowing boats.

Rollerblading In New York people rollerblade
everywhere but no place is better than Central Park
for this exhilarating recreation: there are set routes
for novices, and for the more experienced. For
information see the Braking Clinics at the east and
west street entrances (Page 27 E4 and H4).
The park closes to cars Fris - Mons 19.00 - 6.00 am.
Also January to November 10.00 - 15.00, 19.00 - 22.00

Wildlife Center   H1 31
This zoo is well-loved by New Yorkers. There is an
Arctic Pool with polar bears, Japanese snow
monkeys, red pandas, etc., all woven into a small
area. Perhaps the best to watch are the sea lions in
the central pool. I found the penguins standing and
diving in their man-made Antarctica the most
fascinating - for you can see them under water.
April - October daily 10.00 - 17.00, weekends 10.30 - 17.30
November to March daily 10.00 - 16.30   Charge

RIVERSIDE PARK   Pages 19-20-22-26
Stretching four miles along the shoreline of the
Hudson River. The Park - a jogger's paradise -
provides good walks and views of the river with
many interesting features on the way. The overall
design was by Frederick Law Olmsted; Calvert Vaux
and others also participated. Hollows and hills,
upper-and lower-level walks, playgrounds, numerous
sports facilities, monuments and a yacht marina are
all part of this unique park. As you pass Grant's
Tomb (A2 20 and Page 12), it is interesting to note
that the curved tiled benches that surround the tomb
were constructed by a local residents group. Just
north of this point the views of the Palisades Park
across the river are well worth contemplating.

WASHINGTON SQUARE PARK   G4 39
Not really a park - a square with the famous Roman-
inspired triumphal arch, statues, a fountain (not
always working), dog runs, and stone chess boards.
Up until the 1960's the road ran through the arch
and the center was a turnaround for buses. Today it
is a lively gathering place for students from the
nearby university. The most renowned event in the
park and important for Greenwich Village - which
the park is the focal point of - is the bi-annual
Outdoor Arts Festival which is held in late May-
early June and again in September.

Beaches

New York can get very very hot in summer and
many people need no invitation to laze on a beach.

Orchard Beach   Accessed by Subway Line 6 to
Pelham Bay Park, and then Bus (summer only) 5
or 12 to the beach. Very close by is **City Island**,
connected by Bus 29 from the station, or from
Orchard Beach it is a walk across the causeway. The
island is a haven for nautical enthusiasts and
seafood. Near the bus turnaround is Tito Puente's
restaurant - yes the great Latin timbalist and
vibraphone player. Go midweek, it is less crowded.

Coney Island   Today well past its peak and rather
sad, but it does still have amusement parks and the
New York Aquarium is here. Nearby is Brighton
Beach where lovers of Russian and Ukrainian food
will be well satisfied. Coney Island is reached by
Subway Trains B-D-F or N.

Jacob Riis Park   Located in Queens, this is a nicer
place to swim than Coney Island and you can reach
it by taking the Subway Line A train to Broad
Channel and then the shuttle S to Rockaway Park.

Jones Beach   A Long Island resort famous for
its beach amphitheater where many top stars past
and present perform during summer months.

Fire Island   A 32-mile-long narrow barrier to Long
Island and now a popular party place for the gay
community. Both Long Island beaches are served
by the Long Island Railroad from Penn Station.

THE ARCHITECTURE

Without a Grand Boulevard in view, the essence of New York derives from the spirit of commerce and the great architects of the early 20th century: perhaps the Woolworth building demonstrates this best of all. The construction of the city was not the result of politicians, or generals, or kings, as in Europe, but of self-made men, fulfilling the dreams of all the immigrants who ever set foot in America. Once they succeeded they built places to work from, giant monuments for all to see and aspire to. In 1990 NYC had 25 of the world's tallest buildings.

AMERICAN STANDARD BUILDING   H1 35
40 West 40th Street.   Illuminated at night, the building glows like an enormous coal - reminding you it was built for the American Radiator Co. in 1924. By day, the skyscraper's dark, craggy, neo-Gothic tower looms over the beautifully restored Bryant Park. The black-gold color scheme is most striking: black granite and dark bronze at street level, black brick with terra cotta trim above.
See also the black marble and mirrored lobby.

ANSONIA HOTEL   C4 26
2109 Broadway.   Toscanini, Caruso, and the great Stravinsky once had apartments in this Beaux-Arts gem. Styled in 1904 like a Parisian palace, it reflects the craving for opulent living at that time. Immense ground-floor arches, unusual round corner towers with crowned domes, and a three-story mansard roof are the large scale elements of its grandeur. A wealth of surface detail - decorative railings, rows of ornamental balconies, tiers of windows - make the Ansonia look like a fancy wedding cake.

BROOKLYN BRIDGE   G1 47
Spans East River.   Designed and built by a father-son team, the bridge's completion in 1883 has been called the dawn of modern New York. During the construction many workers and the son of Roebling the designer were crippled by caisson disease (the bends) caused by ascent from deep underwater pressure chambers used to sink the bridge's supports. The magnificent Gothic-inspired towers linked by cables over 15-inches thick and spider-web-like metalwork are breathtaking from afar, but you should walk the 532 yards between the massive stone archways and remember this was the world's first steel-wire suspension bridge. At sunset the view of the New York skyline is terrific. Start your walk in Brooklyn (D3 38).

CHRYSLER BUILDING   C6 32
405 Lexington Avenue. The stainless-steel spire of this 1930 building marks one of the first uses of exposed metal over a large structural surface. The Art Deco-style building is a superb tribute to American automotive excellence: there are abstract automobiles in a decorative band on the 26th floor, enormous winged gargoyles like vintage car radiator caps at the tower base, and a lobby ceiling painted with transit themes. The spire - a pattern of receding arches and triangular windows - was not illuminated until 1981 although it had been in the original plans. Don't miss the Art Deco lobby - a colorful triangle with the city's most famous elevators (with carved-wood cabs, no two alike). The building was financed by Walter Chrysler (1875-1940), an amazing self-made man who began as a machinist: his first tool kit was once displayed in the Cloud Club which used to be on the 71st floor ......This is the jazz age

CITICORP CENTER   C3 33
Lexington Avenue.   This amazing 1978 building with one of the city's finest public spaces seems to hover over a Manhattan block. In fact, it rests on four enormous futuristic aluminum pillars, each centered on the building's four sides. Manhattanites lunch, shop, and feed the birds in the seven-story skylit atrium within. They can even worship at St. Peter's Church, a modern glass-and-granite structure tucked neatly into one of the corners. Above, the steeply sloped profile graces the midtown skyline with its stepped and glinting aluminum surface - show-offy, risky engineering, brilliantly executed!

CITY HALL   F6 43
On City Hall Park. New York's seat of municipal government is a palace. Finished in 1811, this delicately balanced Georgian-style building with French Renaissance detail houses the offices of the Mayor, City Council, and other city agencies. The exterior covered in Alabama veined limestone has rows of arched windows along the facade, a cupola with an illuminated clock (New York's first) and a 6000lb tower bell. At the very top is the statue of *Justice*. The lobby is surpassingly grand. A two-story central rotunda is circled by twin curved marble staircases; they ascend to the second floor landing, where ten Corinthian columns support a huge glass dome. Majestic!
Monday to Friday 10.00 - 16.30   *Free*

DAILY NEWS BUILDING   D6 32
220 East 42nd Street. The lobby houses the world's largest interior globe, an enormous revolving orb illuminated from within and kept meticulously up to date. Lines on the floor point in the directions of cities around the world and to the planets beyond. The piers that project beyond the window wall on the exterior are accentuated by different colors of brick producing a bold vertical stripe effect. The News Building became the *Daily Planet* building for the 1978 *Superman* movie.

EMPIRE STATE BUILDING   A3 36
350 Fifth Avenue. Finished in 1931 at 1250 feet, this was the world's tallest building until 1973. But it was never eclipsed: immortalized in the 1933 movie *King Kong* it still dominates the skyline from any angle. The pale limestone and granite exterior catches light and shadow so subtly that office workers with a view claim it looks different every day and all day long. Its monumental spire designed as a Zeppelin anchorage is now topped by a 222ft TV tower. To take the ride to the 86th floor observatory buy your ticket on the concourse level, passing the lobby where there is some lovely Art Deco detail. One of the building's 73 elevators will lift you swiftly to the promenade deck, where on a clear day you can see over 60 miles in all directions. If you want more, take another elevator to the 102nd floor viewing room. This irresistible building well deserves the description "the cathedral of the skies."   *Charge*
Open daily 9.30 to midnight   (last admission 23.30)

FLATIRON BUILDING   H6 35
175 Fifth Avenue. Named the Fuller building when it was completed in 1902. Popular sentiment forced the owners to call the building shaped like a flat iron just that. Maximizing the triangular space at Fifth and Broadway on Madison Square, the building is rounded off to a width of six feet at its point. Hardly sleek in appearance, in fine Beaux-Arts fashion, the steel frame is covered in limestone and classical ornament from top to bottom. Extremely photogenic and completely unique!

GENERAL ELECTRIC BUILDING   C4 32
570 Lexington Av.   With a brief to blend in with
St. Bartholomew's, the Byzantine style church that
stands alongside. This 1931 building of terra cotta
and bricks merges well: its 51-story octagonal tower
(almost like a pencil) allows room gracefully for
the church. The stylized pinnacles of the tower
assimilate air waves, and remind you that the first
occupants were the RCA Corporation, at that time
a General Electric subsidiary.

GRAND CENTRAL TERMINAL   B6 32
Park Avenue. For some, the most romantic place
in New York. Without, the great facade of 75-foot
arched steel and glass windows, colossal clock,
and Jules Coutan sculpture group faces down Park
Avenue. Within, on the main concourse, you can't
help but look up, up, up into the great, vast space.
Streams of sun fall nine stories from the high east
windows; 2500 stars form the constellations in the
blue vaulted ceiling. On New Year's Eve, when
New Yorkers are invited to waltz in Grand Central,
it seems perfectly fitting. With 33.7 miles of railroad
track on two levels, a subway station, and an
underground shopping concourse, this Beaux-Arts
pearl is an engineering tour de force.

HELMSLEY BUILDING   B5 32
230 Park Av. Built as the HQ of the N.Y. Central
Railroad in 1929, it was the headstone of the great
Classical avenue. Its magnificent tower is topped
by a pyramid roof with Venetian chimneystacks,
and surmounted by a large fanciful lantern. Curved
wings at the base embrace the avenue as two lofty
portals allow traffic to pass. Long before the
malevolent shadow of the Pan Am building rose
up behind it, the extraordinary Helmsley building
was a fitting symbol of the power of the railroads.

METROPOLITAN LIFE Ins., Building   B5 36
1 Madison Avenue. The original building was
erected in 1893, the tower that was to become the
company's symbol and motivate its slogan *The Light
that Never Fails* was added in 1909. Inspired by the
campaniles (oversized bell towers) of North Italy,
the 51-story tower has a high arcade and a steep
sloping roof topped by an ornate lantern. The
huge clock has a minute hand 17ft long. In the
1960's a misguided modernization stripped the
tower of a lot of its ornamental detail, but it
remains impressive, particularly at night, when it
is illuminated in a flood of color visible throughout
New York's night sky.

MUNICIPAL BUILDING   G5 43
Centre Street opposite Chamber Street.
Lovers of architecture have deemed this neoclassic
skyscraper one of America's grandest civic edifices
and the model for any tall building in the Classical
tradition - Moscow University for instance! The
gray granite building is boldly placed, curving in a
shallow U on Centre St. and straddling Chambers
St. with a huge triumphal arch at the center of a
massive Corinthian colonnade. Atop the tower, a
20ft-statue of a woman holds a crown and a shield
(with the city's coat of arms). She is *Civic Fame*
the largest statue on Manhattan Island.

RADIO CITY MUSIC HALL   G4 31
1260 Avenue of the Americas. Originally built as
a vaudeville house, it suffered a long decline, but
it has now been restored to its 1930's Art Deco
elegance. The grand foyer, an entire city block
long, has floor to ceiling mirrors and drapes, two
29ft-long chandeliers, a 24-carat gold leaf ceiling,
and an Ezra Winter mural *Fountain of Youth* behind
the stairs. In the 5874-seat auditorium, a huge
gold arched proscenium - like a sun - rises over
the 144ft stage. A masterpiece of interior design.
If you can't see a show take the Grand Tour.
Mons - Sats 10.00 - 17.00, Suns 11.00 - 17.00

ST. JOHN the DIVINE. Cath.Church of C5 20
Amsterdam Av. Harlem. This Protestant Episcopal
church has been under construction on and off
for over 100 years. Still unfinished - notably the
towers are missing - it is nonetheless the largest
Gothic-styled cathedral in the world, and the largest
church in the U.S. The rose window contains ten
thousand pieces of glass. A mesh of styles, the
older parts Byzantine Romanesque while latterly
more French Gothic in style. The interior is
cavernous. The side aisles are as high as the nave,
and lined with temporary exhibits. But the row of
chapels and its famous organ will literally take
your breath away. This church is renowned for
music, it was here Duke Ellington's *Second Sacred
Concert* was premiered.
Under the care of master masons, local apprentices
are being trained to finish the building. Perhaps
understandably you will be charged admission.

ST. PATRICK'S CATHEDRAL   H4 31
Fifth Avenue. The largest Roman Catholic church
in the U.S. and the seat of the archdiocese of
New York. Begun in 1859 (before the Civil War),
it took 29 years to complete. The white-marble
church is in modified French Gothic style - no
flying buttresses but twin 330ft towers, richly carved.
The spires, the rose window and the three sets of
bronze doors bring a sense of majesty to crowded
Fifth Avenue. Much American history has passed
along the 108ft nave - marriages (F. Scott Fitzgerald
to Zelda in 1928) and funerals (Robert Kennedy
in 1968).

WALDORF-ASTORIA HOTEL   B4 32
301 Park Avenue. Arguably New York's grandest
hotel and residential facility. The original hotel
was torn down to make space for the Empire State,
and this one opened in 1931. An entire block long
with a lobby of restrained Art Deco sophistication
the whole length. The Waldorf's twin copper-clad
towers have been home to Herbert Hoover, General
MacArthur, the Duke of Windsor, Henry Kissinger,
Lucky Luciano, and Cole Porter. Porter's piano
can still be heard in the Peacock Alley restaurant.

WOOLWORTH BUILDING   D1 46
233 Broadway. A dramatic neo-Gothic skyscraper
by Cass Gilbert that some call the most beautiful
commercial building in the world. From 1913 to
1930 it was the tallest. It is resplendent with Gothic
elements: flying buttresses, pointed arches, spires,
vaulted ceilings. Nearly 30 floors of base and 30
floors of tower are covered with terra cotta to
permit elaborate ornamentation - gargoyles and
beasts mythical and real, tracery in the lower stories,
filigree on the tower. Enter the lobby and don't
forget to look up at the vaulted mosaic ceiling. It
sparkles! Frank Woolworth (who appears in a
whimsical lobby sculpture clutching a large nickel)
paid the $13.5 million cost of the building in cash.

WORLD TRADE CENTER   ·C2 46
You should not miss the 90-second trip to the
Observation deck on the 107th floor of the Center's
Tower Two. The twin towers, each a quarter-mile
high, make this the second tallest building in the
world. Although visually boring the 110-story towers
are architecturally innovative: closely spaced vertical
exterior piers bear the load, providing maximum
floor space with no interior columns. The piers
are unrelievedly vertical except for the arches at
ground level and the 107th floor. The wind-swept
central plaza and adjacent areas also have many
harmonious contemporary sculptures; look for Fritz
Koenig's bronze cut-away *Sphere* and Alexander
Calder's red stabile *Three Wings*. The Center
survived a terrorist attack, a car bomb explosion,
on February 28th 1993.
*Observation deck daily October to May 9.30 - 21.30
June to September 9.30 - 23.30*   *Charge*

ENTERTAINMENTS

You can never get bored in New York, it is a fun city full of entertainment arts. All over town events happen. For details get the free *Village Voice* which is published Tuesday every week, or take the Sunday *New York Times* - a huge paper! *Time Out* publish a listing magazine and there are numerous free papers - usually found on street corners in metal boxes or your hotel lobby - with the week's selections.

Concert Halls

BROOKLYN ACADEMY OF MUSIC
30 Lafayette Street   © *718/636 4100*
Americans like acronyms and BAM this institution is affectionately called. Built in a neo-Italianate style in 1908, the building has three spaces which serve the performing arts, including: an opera house, a small chamber music room and a symphony hall where the Brooklyn Philharmonic are the resident orchestra. This opera house is where Enrico Caruso suffered a severe throat haemorrhage on stage during a performance on the 11th December 1920. He died seven months later in his birthplace, Naples. Today the Academy is famed for its innovations and New Wave Festival.
Subway Line 2 - 3 or 4 to Atlantic Avenue.

CARNEGIE HALL   F2 31
Corner 57th Street, Seventh Avenue   © *247 7800*
Lovingly restored back to its original appearance and redesigned to include the Weill Recital Hall and a cinema. This is the most cherished concert hall in the United States: renowned for ambience and quality of sound but not that comfortable in the first tier from my own experience. Built between 1889 and 1891 and since that time almost every notable in classical music has played here: Tchaikovsky, Resphigi, Saint-Saens, Mahler, Ravel, Prokofiev, Gershwin, Ellington, Copland, and Dvorak who premiered his New World Symphony here in 1893 - the list is endless. Located on the second floor is the small Rose Museum open during performances and to the public 11.00 - 16.30 but not on Wednesdays. It is an interesting display of memorabilia relating to the artists who have given unforgettable performances here: posters, programs, batons, records and even Benny Goodman's clarinet are on display. Not only classical but the great jazz and popular artists who have performed in the hall are featured: Edith Piaf, Judy Garland, the Beatles, Frank Sinatra, Miles Davis, and Charlie Parker with Strings, etc.
Tours of the hall, performance permitting. *Charge Mons, Tues, Thurs, Fris at 11.30, 14.00 and at 15.00*

LINCOLN CENTER   D6 26
One of the most popular entertainment places in the city and the largest of its kind in the United States. Other venues in the center will be described in their appropriate sections.
Avery Fisher Hall   © *875 5030*
Rebuilt several times in an attempt to improve the acoustics. This has been achieved by altering the shape as well as other design improvements. This is the home of the New York Philharmonic. America's oldest orchestra, and I don't mean visually! Leonard Bernstein spent ten years of his

BARGEMUSIC   A1 48
Fulton Ferry Landing, Brook. © *718/624 4061*
Throughout the year, twice weekly chamber music concerts take place close by Brooklyn Bridge on a barge, and you have that great romantic view as a backdrop. *Thurs and Suns.*

life with this orchestra but he was overtaken by Zubin Mehta who stayed from 1977 to 1991. The orchestra is famed for its Mostly Mozart Festival which is an annual event.

Opera and Ballet

Perhaps equalling jazz, the other great creative musical associated art that has flourished in New York is ballet: Martha Graham and Alvin Ailey are legends and there is no doubt that Arthur Mitchel and Merce Cunningham will be.

CITY CENTER THEATER   G3 31
131 West 55th Street   © *581 1212*
A former temple building with a Moorish facade that was saved from extinction in 1943 by Mayor LaGuardia. Throughout the year modern American ballet troupes take the stage here, including most of the ones in my introduction.

JOYCE THEATER   D1 38
175 Eighth Avenue.   © *242 0800*
A converted 40's cinema located in Chelsea from which the Feld Ballet operates: Eliot Feld has choreographed the great American composers. He is a 20th-century choreographer with great reverence for the past: if you saw the film of *West Side Story* you have seen him.

NEW YORK STATE THEATER   D1 30
Lincoln Center   © *870 5570*
This classical-inspired building which seats 2738 people is considered to be the best on the site. It features opera and ballet, and is where the late George Balanchine's NYC Ballet perform. One of Balanchine's early assignments when he arrived in New York in 1933 was to choreograph *Slaughter on Tenth Avenue* for the Rodgers and Hart show *On Your Toes*. Many people hold the opinion that Balanchine created the American style of ballet and this world-class troupe is his legacy.

METROPOLITAN OPERA HOUSE   D6 26
Lincoln Center   © *362 6000*
The home of the revered opera company that gives its name to the building: its reputation was built from 1883 to 1966 in the old opera house that stood in the heart of the Theater District on Broadway, between 39th and 40th, before it was demolished. Today this modern opera house faces the Columbus Avenue approach to the Center: it is not as flamboyant as Sydney or as austere as the Bastille. In the entrance are murals by Marc Chagall and great crystal chandeliers in the lobby and the hall, which rise to the ceiling when a performance is about to start on its massive stage. It is very expensive and the cheap seats are very high up. Accommodating over 3780 people, it is the largest auditorium on the site.
The opera also shares the stage with the American Ballet Theater, a group formed in 1939 in the classic ballet tradition but in recent years branching into more modern choreography under the artistic direction of the Russian Mikhail Baryshnikov. In the 1980's many controversial interpretations of ballets old and new were performed.
Tours of the Center are daily from 10.00 -17.00 and last one hour. For details © *(212) 875 5350.* There is also a back-stage tour of the Opera House that explores the stage complex, auditorium, production shops and dressing rooms.
Weekdays at 15.45, and on Saturdays at 10.00
Charge   *For reservations* © *(212) 769 7020.*

Theaters

Theater - well this is the place - the only rival is perhaps London's Shaftesbury Avenue. But nothing matches the magic of an opening on Broadway, as most actors will tell you. There is not enough room here to detail every theater so here is my selection that includes some of the great theaters and others that might be of interest for their productions.

CORT THEATRE   **G5 31**
134 West 48th Street   ℂ Telecharge *239 6200*
Built in 1912, over the years many great stars and plays have been premiered in this delightful French style theater/palace. At the end of the 40's Katherine Hepburn started her love affair with Shakespeare in *As You Like It* on this stage.

DOUGLAS FAIRBANKS THEATRE   **D6 30**
432 West 42nd Street   ℂ *239 4321*
This off Broadway, small, alternative, comfortable theater is approached through a small courtyard behind Theater Row. It is well known for the musical *Nunsense* that ran for many years.

IMPERIAL THEATER   **E5 31**
249 West 45th Street   ℂ Telecharge *239 6200*
Opened in 1923 and built by the Shubert Brothers, it has a very elegant interior with good views from most seats. Known for its great revues and musicals: *Rose Marie* was premiered here, and Gene Kelly and Mary Martin captured Broadway on this stage.

LYCEUM   **F5 31**
149 West 45th Street   ℂ Telecharge *239 6200*
This is New York's oldest theater and it is well worth a diversion for its architecture: ornate with a wave-like porch (marquee) and strong intaglio columns and with interior marble staircases, it has a Beaux-Arts appeal about it. When it was built in 1903 it introduced cantilevered balconies, doing away with columns that obstructed views. Many great stars have played this theater, but I would most of all have liked to have seen Judy Holliday in *Born Yesterday* when it opened here in 1946.

MAJESTIC   **E6 31**
245 West 44th Street   ℂ Telecharge *239 6200*
With over 1700 comfortable seats this theater is a natural choice for handling very large scale musical productions, which it has done since 1927.

NEW AMSTERDAM   **F6 31**
214 West 42nd Street.
In this theater dreams were made - the glorious *Ziegfeld's Follies* and George White's *Scandals* both adorned this stage. The Disney organization is due to renovate the theater and hopefully will return it to its former Art-Nouveau grandeur and perhaps even the roof garden theater will return.

PALACE THEATRE   **F5 31**
1564 Broadway   ℂ Ticketmaster *307 4100*
You have heard Judy sing the song......this is the place. You were made in vaudeville if you played the Palace, and since 1913 all the legends have played here. The exterior of the building has gone but the original auditorium remains surrounded by a hotel/office block. A cinema for several years, today it is a good center for musical shows.

RADIO CITY MUSIC HALL   **G4 31**
Rockefeller Center   ℂ Ticketmaster *307 7171*
Without doubt if there is one entertainment venue that you should see, this is it. I cannot believe that they considered demolishing it. A twentieth-century dream......superb.   See Page 51

> **Broadway Line** for current information on Broadway plays and musicals ℂ *(212) 563 2929*

SULLIVAN STREET PLAYHOUSE   **G6 39**
181 Sullivan Street   ℂ *674 3838*
An intimate little theater in the heart of Greenwich Village where *The Fantasticks* has been playing forever - May 1963: this has become an institution almost like *The Mousetrap* in London is.

WINTER GARDEN   **F4 31**
1634 Broadway   Telecharge ℂ *239 6200*
The theater that introduced Al Jolson to Broadway with the famous runway that bridged the pit. Fanny Brice also played on this stage and *Funny Girl,* the musical based on her life, was a natural to be produced at this theater.

Movie Theaters - Cinemas

Whats showing at the Roxy? Nothing - this 6000-seat theater was demolished in 1961 as were numerous other glorious fantasy palaces. But the dreams go on and New York has many cinemas, very much like anywhere else now - multiplex. New York gets the films first so here are a few theaters which will not disappoint you.

ANGELIKA FILM CENTER   **H6 39**
18 West Houston Street   ℂ *995 2000*
A popular cinema not far from Greenwich Village with six screens that features independent and foreign films mostly.

ASTOR PLAZA   **F6 31**
44th Street   ℂ *869 8340*
Almost on Times Square, this auditorium with one very large screen is embedded in an office tower: the developers had to build a cinema thanks to the area improvement organization BID.

WALTER READE THEATER   **D6 26**
Lincoln Center   ℂ *875 5600*
This theater shows independent and foreign films on a very large screen with superb sound. If you cannot get tickets or afford the opera, ballet or music programs then browse around the center and take in a movie.

ZIEGFELD   **G3 31**
141 West 54th Street   ℂ *765 7600*
This is the one, a massive screen (one of the largest in the US), very luxurious, comfortable and with beautiful surroundings. The ideal place to see a new movie.

Ticket Agencies

Advance tickets can be booked at theaters or on:

TICKETMASTER   ℂ *307 7171*
TELECHARGE   ℂ *239 6200*

TKTS operate two ticket booths where you can obtain same day tickets with a 25% or 50% discount for cash or traveler's checks only.
Duffy Square, Broadway   **F5 31**
15.00 - 20.00, Matinees on Weds, Sats 11.00 - 15.30
2 World Trade Center, mezzanine level   **C2 46**

Reduced-price tickets for concerts - recitals can be obtained from the booth in Bryant Park. **G6 31**

Two-Fers Visitors can obtain two tickets for the price of one from the Visitors' Bureau which is located at Columbus Circle.   **E2 31**

> **MADISON SQUARE GARDEN**   **F3 35**
> Penn Plaza Drive   ℂ *465 5800*
> There are two venues in the Garden: the arena that holds 20,000 and the smaller 4600 seat **Paramount**, both hold pop and rock concerts as well as boxing, circuses and exhibitions.

SPORTS

TENNIS For years Forest Hills in Queens was the scene of the US Open Tennis Championship, but this changed in 1978 when the open which is held in late August moved to the Louis Armstrong Stadium, Flushing Meadows (Louis who died in 1971, lived nearby). The stadium unfortunately is under a flight path to La Guardia airport.
Subway Line 7 to Willetts Point/Shea Stadium.
The All Women's Virginia Slims Championship is held in Madison Sq. Garden (F3 35) in November.

BASEBALL April to September is the baseball season and New York is where the game was developed in the 19th century. Whether you sit in the bleachers or in expensive seats it is well worth a visit. The Yankee Stadium in the Bronx opened in 1923 and is the most famous stadium in the US. It is the home of the great Yankees who from the 1920's dominated the game and are arguably the greatest club in the history of the sport: outstanding past members include Lou Gehrig, Babe Ruth, Mickey Mantle and Joe DiMaggio the player who married Marilyn Monroe.
Subway C - D or 4 to Yankee Stadium/161 Street.
It is unfortunate the Brooklyn Dodgers are no longer: after the season of 1957 they moved to Los Angeles. They will go down in the sports history as the first team to field a black player, the inspirational and much-revered Jackie Robinson.
The only other National League team that resides in NYC is the New York Mets, who are based at the Shea Stadium in Queens near Flushing Meadows, Corona Park. The club was formed in in 1962 and filled the gap the Dodgers had left. On the way to or from JFK airport you have probably seen the sphere left over from the World's Fair of 1964-5, this is Flushing Meadows Park and Shea Stadium is just to the north.
Subway Line 7 to Willets Point/Shea Stadium.
In case either of the teams are featured, the finals of the World Series - a seven-match play-off between the winners of the two top leagues - takes place at the end of the season.

FOOTBALL Not the European variety which is called soccer in the US, but the full-blooded American variety. This season starts in September and goes through to the end of December and terminates with the Super-Bowl play-offs. New York has two teams, the NY Giants and the NY Jets, who both play across the Hudson River in East Rutherford, New Jersey, in the Giants Stadium which is part of the vast Meadowlands Sports complex. The best way to reach the stadium is by bus from the Port Authority Bus Terminal (E1 35).

BASKETBALL Although the city is full of playground pitches this is an indoor sport played from October to May. The venue for the famous NY Knickerbockers (the Knicks) is Madison Square Garden (F3 35) where they alternate with the Rangers ice hockey team. When in town the famous touring Harlem Globetrotters can also be seen occasionally at the Garden.

HORSE RACING The Runyon stories have always given me the impression that the city had a love affair with racing, guys on street corners in striped suits studying form. Indeed racing does go back to 1665 when a track for thoroughbred horses was established on Long Island.
There are three great races in American flat racing that comprise the triple crown: the Belmont Stakes, Preakness Stakes and of course the Kentucky Derby. The Belmont Stakes (1867) are held on the third Saturday in June at Belmont Park in Elmont,

Long Island, just across the boundary line of Queens in Nassau County, NE of JFK airport.
To reach Belmont Park where flat racing is held from May to July and September to mid October your best bet is to catch the Belmont Special which leaves Penn Station (F3 35) every 20 minutes from 9.45 until midday on race days.
During August racing goes up state New York to Saratoga Springs which is some distance from the city and is near the state capital, Albany.
The other New York racetrack is the Aqueduct course where racing is held from October to May in Ozone Park which is 30 minutes by Express Subway. *Line A to Aqueduct/North Conduit Avenue.*

MANHATTAN DISTRICTS

CHELSEA Pages 34 - 35. An area with an increasing gay community which includes the 'Flower District' between 27th and 30th Streets on Sixth Avenue. The famous Chelsea Hotel (E6 35) has been home to many famous literary figures and artists.

GARMENT DISTRICT Page 35. Fashion Avenue is the name given to Seventh Avenue where it runs through the bespoke center of the US. Here too is Madison Square Garden directly over Penn Station, the busiest terminal in North America.

GREENWICH VILLAGE Page 39. The spiritual center of the village is Washington Square. This colorful area - the lowlands of Manhattan - has beckoned artists of all descriptions for years. Full of restaurants, cafes and jazz clubs, its al fresco art exhibitions and Halloween costume parade are annual highlights.

GRAMERCY PARK Page 36. A neighborhood on the east side of Manhattan containing the small private park reminiscent of a London garden square. Pete's Tavern (est. 1864) is close by on Irving Place and has a restaurant and sidewalk cafe. James Cagney lived on the park and actor John Garfield was found dead in mysterious circumstances at No. 3, also facing the park.

HARLEM Page 21. Once a Jewish enclave, but since the early 1900s a magnet attracting black people from all over the US and the world. A source for black intellectuals, jazz musicians, entertainers and sports personalities. Sugar Hill (D1 19) is where the more wealthy aspired to live, and El Barrio (C1 24) is the name for Hispanic Harlem.

LOWER EAST SIDE Pages 44-45. Part of this area includes Little Italy and Chinatown. Once a breeding ground for entertainment personalities like the Gershwins, Eddie Cantor, Irving Berlin and Al Jolson. Many people experienced life here once they got off the boat.

Chinatown Pages 43-44. The largest Chinese population in the US now encompasses 35 blocks and Lower Mott Street is its center. The streets brim with activity and pungent Oriental aromas.

Little Italy Page 43. Although receding due to its neighbor Chinatown pushing westwards, the center is Mulberry Street and it is here in mid-September that the ten-day San Gennaro Festival takes place.

SOHO Page 43 The name derives from 'South of Houston' (House-ton). Renowned for its cast iron loft buildings, art galleries and designer boutiques.

TRIBECA Page 43. Another acronym, the 'Triangle below Canal' street. Once warehouses and factories: today it is emerging as a trendy place with many buildings converted to residential lofts. The Tribeca Film Center is based above the *Tribeca Grill.*

INTERESTING WALKS

A Downtown Walk

In 1624, the tip of Manhattan became home to the island's first European settlers, a Dutch colony called New Amsterdam, a tiny community bordered by Wall Street to the north (it was actually a wall then, to keep out the British), Broadway to the west and Water Street to the east. Despite the wall, the British took over with hardly a fight in 1664 and ruled until the Revolution. The original Federal Hall briefly reigned as capital of the new nation with the banks and the Stock Exchange for neighbors, and what became in the 18th century the world's busiest port on its doorstep. Today the financial district still remains where it began. We start our walk at **Bowling Green** (D4 46) which in 1733 was the city's first public park, and where a statue of King George III of England stood in gratitude for his repeal of a loathsome tax (after independence it was knocked down). See today's statue, *Charging Bull* - in Stock Exchange terms a bull is an optimist!

A few steps into **Battery Park** and you see the Netherlands Memorial Flagpole commemorating the dubious $24 deal struck between the Dutch and the local Indians. The name Battery Park comes from the British who kept a battery of guns here to protect the harbor. After the Revolution a 22-acre park was created, but the park returned to its warlike origins when **Castle Clinton** was built, anticipating the war of 1812 (see Page 11).

Along the **Admiral Dewey Promenade**, you will find one of New York's best views. Note to your left Governor's Island which is occupied by the Coast Guard. Close to the shore on your right, partly submerged, is the Merchant Mariners Memorial honoring heroes of World War II. When leaving the park walk toward the blue glass skyscraper (17 State Street), to the free museum of urban archaeology, **New York Unearthed**, where New York's past is revealed in what is buried underground. Next door is a beautiful brick building, a shrine to the first American-born saint, St. Elizabeth Bayley Seton, a wealthy widow who converted to Catholicism and founded the first Catholic school. This part of State Street was once lined with graceful Federal townhouses (see inside cover). Follow Water Street to Bedford Street and turn left to find the **Fraunces Tavern**, whose historical significance is noted on Page 9; it is also a restaurant, *open Monday - Friday 7.00 - 21.30*. Head back to Bowling Green, following Bridge Street to Whitehall. Across from the subway station is the splendid **U.S. Custom House**, a 1907 building held to be the grandest Beaux-Arts edifice in the city (now the Museum of the American Indian see Page 8). Four monumental limestone sculptures that represent four continents, by Daniel Chester French (who also sculpted the Lincoln in the Lincoln Memorial), stand white against the gray granite. Do look inside at the rotunda and the large oval mural depicting *An Ocean Liner Entering New York Harbor*.

The walk follows Broadway, where some of the city's most fabulous classical skyscrapers are found. The **Cunard Building** (1921) at No. 25 (now the Post Office) housed the steamship company with the fastest luxury liners in the world. See the glorious octagonal, domed Great Hall. Across the street is the old **Standard Oil Building**, a unique because it curves along Broadway, but has a tower squared to the grid of the city. Another striking aspect is the application of classical elements three-

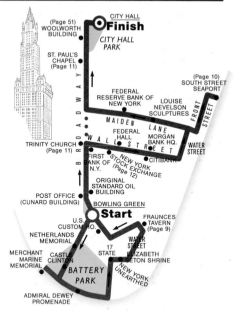

story Ionic columns appear high up the base of the building, and are repeated on all four sides of the tower, which is crowned by an unusual stepped pyramid with a colossal tripod from which steam or smoke emit, as if in sacrifice to the gods.

An Anglican church has stood where Broadway meets Wall Street since 1698, making **Trinity Church** and churchyard one of the earliest churches in America (see Page 11). It is undoubtedly the loveliest spot in lower Manhattan. A brownstone building with a 284-foot spire and a graveyard with such notable figures as Alexander Hamilton, the man who launched the American economy.

Turn right onto Wall Street, NYC's financial row, note the **Bank of New York's** 1797 cornerstone and the **New York Stock Exchange** (see Page 12) and **Federal Hall** (Page 11) which commemorates the first building on the site. The glass-and-granite-striped **Morgan Bank** tower (1989) further down is an attempt to relate to its older neighbors.

A left on Water Street takes you to Maiden Lane where a right jag to Front Street leads you to the **South Street Seaport**, a nice lunch spot if you are hungry. See page 10 for more details.

Returning along Maiden Lane you will reach Nevelson Plaza, where seven sculptures by abstract artist Louise Nevelson were raised in 1978. Just past the plaza is a checkerboard pattern fortress the **Federal Reserve** Bank of New York. Deep beneath this building lies more gold than anywhere else on earth, belonging to more than 80 countries. Returning to Broadway walk north to see New York's only building predating the Revolutionary War **St. Paul's Chapel** (see Page 11); then the **Woolworth Building** built in 1913 and the jewel in the crown of Manhattan's commercial skyline (see Page 51); and **City Hall**, my vote for the most graceful and airy building design (see Page 50).

Lower East Side Walk

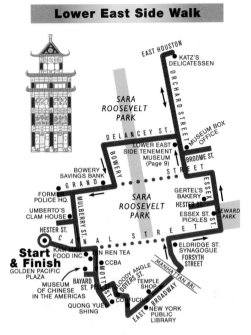

They say America is a 'melting pot' of different cultures; well, NYC is more like a crock pot set on simmer. With neighborhoods and business areas dominated by diverse immigrant groups, no one seems in any hurry to assimilate. In the 19th century the Lower East Side contained the city's worst slums. Irish, Italians, East European Jews and Chinese made their first home in the crowded tenements. Today Chinatown dominates the area, but remnants of other groups remain. We start our walk in Chinatown, then visit the remains of the Jewish presence and end up in Little Italy.

Beginning at Canal Street, one of the city's busiest streets, dominated by Chinese-owned businesses. This is the living vibrant Chinatown. at 200 Canal is **Kam Man Food Inc.**, a two-floor supermarket worth a look if you like exotic food. The turn onto Mott Street leads into Old Chinatown, and at No.75 on your right is the modern **Ten Ren Tea & Ginseng** shop where you can buy tea to take home. Across the street at No. 62 is the **Chinese Consolidated** Benevolent Association, which unofficially ran Chinatown for 100 years and provides a service to new immigrants. It is not to be confused with the tongs, secret societies or gangs. At Bayard Street turn right for the **Museum of Chinese in the Americas** (G4 43) situated on the corner at 70 Mulberry St., this museum recalls and explains the Chinese experience in America from its earliest days.

Open from Tuesday to Sunday 10.30 - 17.00. Charge
Returning to Mott Street, which is lined with shops, but none as old as **Quong Yuen Shing & Co.** at No 32, founded in 1891, which sells sandalwood soap, silk handkerchiefs, abacuses and a complete set of Judge Dee mysteries by Robert Van Gulik. Retrace your steps back to Pell Street and then the turn onto Doyers, brings you to the heart of Old Chinatown. In scale and mood, the streets look unchanged for decades. The crook in Doyers

Street was once known as 'Bloody Angle', because two rival *tongs* engaged in a forty-year-long war frequently shed blood at this turn. You will return abruptly to the present when Doyers Street lets you out onto Chatham Square, where on one corner stands a large **Statue of Confucius**. The building on the square that looks like a Chinese temple is in fact the Republic National Bank.

Follow East Broadway a few blocks out of the square, this is rather an ugly commercial stretch, mostly Chinese, but you might peek in at the storefront Grace Gratitude Buddhist Temple at No. 48, visitors are welcome. Across the street is the Public Library (B4 44), which contains a very large Chinese Heritage collection - 10,000 titles in Chinese and English exploring the Chinese experience in America.

Just past the Manhattan Bridge approach, turn left onto Forsyth Street then into Eldridge. You will see the **Eldridge Street Synagogue** on the right. Built in 1887, the first synagogue built by East European (Polish) Jews in America. The first Jews to arrive in New York were Spanish and Portugese from South America. Quite often mistaken for a cathedral this lovely Moorish/Gothic -style building is now being restored.

Tours on Sundays 12.00 - 16.00, and on weekdays by appointment only.   *Charge*
At the top of the block, turn right and follow Canal Street to Essex Street, where shops selling everything from pickles to prayer shawls give a last glimpse of the old Jewish Lower East Side. **Zelig Blumenthal's** at No. 13 is a religious article shop. At 35 is the now-famous **Essex Street Pickles**, better known as Guss's and featured in the film *Crossing Delancey*, and offering pickles, olives, pickled tomatoes, horseradish, etc. The barrels are plastic now, but the sign is the same: 'Please keep hands out of barrels'. Just off Essex on Hester No. 53 is **Gertel's Bakery**, for excellent challah, rugelach, and pumpernickel and coffee. Continue up Essex Street, turning left at Grand, walk two blocks and turn right (north) for the **Lower East Side Tenement Museum** (B2 44) at 90 Orchard Street (Page 9 Museums). If you now feel like some classic New York deli food take the detour up Orchard Street to 205 East Houston (D6 40) **Katz's Delicatessen** established in 1889. Now renowned as the scene of Sally's faked orgasm in the film *When Harry Met Sally*. Remember? - 'I'll have what she's having!'

If you skip the detour, follow Orchard Street to Delancey, turn left, and left again at Bowery, go south and then right into Grand Street where you can see the old **Bowery Savings Bank**, designed in 1894 in American Classical Revival style. Further down Grand Street on the right is an impressive block, once the Police Headquarters (G3 43).

What is left of **Little Italy** mingles with Chinatown. Italian immigrants dominated this area in the early 20th century. Today, most Italian businesses are clustered around Mulberry Street between Canal and Prince Streets and on Grand. In mid-September many Italian Americans return for the San Gennaro Festival, which honors the patron saint of Naples. Allegations of Mafia control of the festival have threatened it in recent years, reminding one of the area's history as headquarters of the Italian mob. In 1972, gangster Joey Gallo was shot to death while having a family dinner at **Umberto's Clamhouse**, (G3 43) located on the corner of Hester at 129 Mulberry Street.

This is the end of the walk and an excellent spot for dinner. Notice that many restaurants display photographs of their famous clientele. The choice is yours but you could try Il Cortile at 125 Mulberry Street for garden dining or the long-established Vincent's (H3 43), unless you feel like clams!

A Greenwich Village Walk

New Yorkers don't agree on much, but many will admit that Greenwich Village is their favorite neighborhood. The historic village, once part of a vast Dutch tobacco plantation and then a British farm, is still preserved in the winding streets and small scale of the buildings. The village was briefly home to the American aristocrats who people Henry James's and Edith Wharton's novels - but it is best known as Little Bohemia. Since the 19th century the Village has welcomed students, artists, writers, musicians, from Washington Irving to Bob Dylan. This free lifestyle has spread clear across town to Avenue C. The cheap rents are no more, but the West Village is still the cafe, live music, and off-Broadway theater center of NYC. We start at **Washington Square Park** the heart of the Village, and view first the elegantly proportioned **Arch** (see Page 12) then look across at the row of Greek Revival townhouses 1-13 on the north side of the square between Fifth Avenue and University Place, the finest surviving row of 19c buildings in the city. Number 3 was renovated into studios where the great American artists Rockwell Kent and Edward Hopper painted, and at number 18 Henry James's grandmother lived. His time spent here as a boy inspired James's novel *Washington Square*. Double back up Fifth Avenue to view the gated block called **Washington Mews**, this is where the stables and gardens of the grand houses used to be. Author of *USA*, John Dos Passos lived at 20a. The 300-year-old elm tree at the north-west corner of the park was at one time known as the **Hanging Elm**, where a local hangman performed his unpleasant work. Behind the square is another 'mews' **MacDougal Alley**. The heiress Gertrude Vanderbilt Whitney lived among her artist friends here, supporting them by buying their work. Her personal collection became the nucleus of the Whitney Museum of American Art.

Look up Sixth Avenue at the red-brick building which is topped by a 150-foot clocktower. This is **Jefferson Market Library**, built in 1876 on the site of a former meat market, and originally a courthouse. The adjoining landscaped garden was created after the annex (a women's jail) was demolished. Off Waverly Place is a charming block called **Gay Street**. A row of speakeasies in the 20s, Gay Street's fortunes changed when Ruth McKenney arrived from Ohio and lived at No.14 with her sister and wrote their adventures in the *New Yorker*. The tales became a play and a musical, and a movie *My Sister Eileen* with Rosalind Russell. At the odd intersection where Waverly Place meets Christopher Street stands the triangular-shaped **Northern Dispensary**, built in 1831, and then the most northerly medical facility in Manhattan. Along Christopher Street are or were some of the Village's most famous bars, including at No. 59 the **Lion's Head**, where Jimmy Breslin and Norman Mailer drank; and at 53 **Stonewall Inn**, a gay bar where a 1969 police raid prompted a riot that launched the gay rights movement in America. Across the street lies **Christopher Park** where alongside General Sheridan there are statues by George Segal that honor gay and lesbian love. Near Sheridan Square are two major off-Broadway theaters, **Circle in the Square** and further down Christopher Street the **Lucille Lortel**. At number **11 Commerce Street** lived Washington Irving

of 'Rip Van Winkle' fame. Just before the crook in Commerce St. is **Cherry Lane Theater** founded by poet Edna St. Vincent Millay in 1926. *Waiting for Godot* by Samuel Becket was premiered here. Across the street from the elegant 1831 mansard-roofed houses at 39 and 41 Commerce is the **Grange Hall**, an excellent bar and restaurant which retains a 1940's feel. At Barrow St. turn left and walk to Hudson St., then northwards to the third oldest church in Manhattan **St. Luke in the Fields** (1822). The first warden was Clement Clarke Moore, whose first year here was spent composing the poem that started, "Twas the night before Christmas......" Half a block up Grove Street on your right is **Grove Court**, six beautiful Greek Revival houses built between 1848 and 1854 (visible behind a locked gate), and until 1921 known as Mixed Ale Alley, reflecting the residents' habits. On the corner of Bedford Street at 17 Grove Street is a large wood-frame house dating from 1822, and you cannot miss **Twin Peaks**, the white fairy-tale-like building at the rear, the happy result of a 1925 renovation. **Chumley's**, behind an unmarked door at 86 Bedford Street, is a lively village bar. Opened in 1926 as a speakeasy, there is a hidden exit in Pamela Court, a tiny alleyway around the corner at 58 Barrow street, Chumley's in its early days was another writers' bar, and its famous patrons' book jackets proudly line the walls: John Dos Passos, F. Scott Fitzgerald, Eugene O'Neill and later the Beats, including Jack Kerouac. **Isaacs-Hendricks House** (1799) at 77 Bedford Street is the oldest house in the Village, and 75½ Bedford, at nine-and-a-half feet the narrowest house in the city: Edna St. Vincent Millay lived here. A block south of Bedford is Leroy Street, a rather nondescript street which curves and magically becomes **St. Luke's Place**, a really lovely block of Italianate brownstones with a fair share of literary history. During 1922-3 Theodore Dreiser wrote *An American Tragedy* at number 16. Poet Marianne Moore lived at No. 14 for ten years, the last three as editor of *The Dial* the avant garde Village literary journal. Sherwood Anderson, author of the classic *Winesburg, Ohio*, lived in a basement apartment at No. 12 in 1923. Finally across the street, the now **Jimmy Walker Park** (the songwriter-mayor lived at No.6), was a cemetery which inspired Edgar Allan Poe's 1838 *The Narrative of Arthur Gordon Pym*. We finish at appropriately the **Anglers & Writers** for tea or perhaps a delicious home-baked pie.

PEACE IN THE BRONX

Over the years the southern Bronx has achieved quite a reputation, notorious would seem an appropriate way to describe it, but there is no need to worry about going to the places mentioned here: these are peaceful escapes where New Yorkers' take their families. You may not realize it, but you are on the mainland when you arrive in the Bronx: it is in fact the only one of New York's five boroughs that is part of the mainland.

NEW YORK ZOOLOGICAL PARK (Bronx Zoo)

The cheapest and most direct way to reach the zoo is by Subway Line No.2 to Pelham Parkway and then walk west to the Bronxdale entrance.

Liberty Lines operate an air-conditioned bus from mid-Manhattan that also takes you to the Bronxdale entrance, for details of this express service BXM 11 telephone (718) 652 8400 for fares, schedules and the stops on Madison Avenue.

This really is a great zoo, the best in New York: the largest city zoo in the United States and one of the world's finest. I was amazed to see deer grazing a few feet away from two lions - thats how good the illusion is - for there are deep trenches or moats which separate them, but they are not visible from many of the viewing positions. The park is home to over 4000 animals and they are in habitats that are more natural than you will find in many zoos.

When you arrive you will get a zoo plan with your admission ticket which will give you the latest information on what is going on in the zoo. Once in the entrance, try to reach the Fountain Circle, which should be the starting point for your safari through the park's 265 acres. On your way to the Circle detour through the tropical rainforest of the World of Birds, with cockatoos, birds of paradise and even simulated thunderstorms. Reaching the Fountain Circle, go up the steps and walk towards the sea lion pool where on each side are the zoo's original buildings and cages, now silent and empty of hungry animals. This is where they used to keep some of the more ferocious species. Now they are administration buildings and the animals are in more humane surroundings, which we enter like 'Mowgli' to learn from them.

For me the highlight of the zoo are the lowland gorilla families. The gorillas always seem to be weighing you up as much as you are them. At this moment there are sixteen (including twins) in two families: by the year 2000 this will be doubled once the Congo Gorilla Forest opens. Over 400 species consisting of 20,000 plants will be planted. One feature is going to be a walk through a deep forested pathway which will have a subterranean tunnel partly enclosed in a thin curtain of glass.

Make sure you visit the Himalayan Highlands where you can get a glimpse of the endangered snow leopard. Africa comes complete with African mud architecture - the Somba Village. Jungle World places you inside the habitat of gibbons, tapirs, crocodiles, etc. Wild Asia can only be viewed principally between May and October from the Bengali Express - a monorail - that takes you through forests and meadows where elephants, rhinos, deer and Siberian tigers roam free. In summer months there are also camel rides, a zoo shuttle and skyfari (an aerial tramway) that runs from Wild Asia above the enclosures to the Children's Zoo.

Open Daily at 10.00.
Closing Times: Monday to Friday 17.00.
Weekends and public holidays 17.30.
November to February 10.00 - 16.30.   *Charge*
On Wednesday admission is free.

NEW YORK BOTANICAL GARDEN

Although just across the Fordham Road, north of the zoo's Rainey Gate, it is some distance away from any of the garden entrances. The best approach is by the Metro North railroad, Botanical Gardens Station. You can get this train from Grand Central Station, but do note the time of the train you wish to return on. I would advise you not to do the zoo and garden on the same day. The garden really is a peaceful haven, quite remote from the bustle and thrust of Manhattan: it should be enjoyed when you need peace and rest from other matters and you have the time to walk without too much haste.

Although very much inspired by London's Kew Gardens it is in fact in a more scenic setting: for the park contains the picturesque gorge of the Bronx river and several historic buildings which were here before the 240 acres of parkland were created by state legislature in 1891.

The southern side of the park opposite the zoo's main entrance is the wildest part of the park and is partly conifer forest. The old Lorillard Snuff Mill (1840), powered by water from the Bronx river, once used to grind tobacco into powdered snuff; today it is a cafe with a pleasant terrace close by one of the gardens picnic areas. Further north up the river, near the forest entrance, is the arched stone Hester Bridge from where the river gorge can be viewed.

The Haupt Conservatory houses an Orangerie and a Palm Court, and is very much like a Victorian glass conservatory. Thankfully preserved, it has eleven pavilions which reach round two pools that contain aquatic plants.

When you enter the park you will be able to get leaflets on various seasonal happenings in the park. Very close to the entrance is the Museum building where there is a library, an indoor center, an orchid terrarium and a garden shop.

To orientate yourself take the tram tour which has a commentary and allows you to get off and board at various points: it runs every 25 minutes.
Tuesday to Sunday and holidays.
April to October 10.00 - 18.00.
November to March 10.00 - 16.00.   *Charge*
Free Wednesday all day and Saturday 10.00-12.00

WAVE HILL   675 West 252nd Street, Bronx.

The easiest approach is by the Metro North line to Riverdale Station from Grand Central Station the entrance is in Independence Avenue opposite 249 Street West.

Deeded to the City of New York in 1960, this pastoral estate is located in the pleasant and affluent suburb of Riverdale. It overlooks the Hudson river and is opposite the New Jersey Palisades Park. The Bronx in this locality has many trees and the 28-acre Wave Hill estate includes an arboretum as well as a public garden. The mansion built in 1843 has an adjoining Armor Hall (1928), and below this and built in 1910, there is a recreation center and a bowling alley. Once the residence of the UK's ambassador to the United Nations; other residents have included Theodore Roosevelt, Samuel Clemens (Mark Twain) and Arturo Toscanni.

Open Tuesdays to Sundays 9.00 - 17.30.
Mid October - mid May 9.00 - 16.30.
Free Tuesday - Friday. Sats and Sundays.   *Charge*

> Did you know Teddy Bears were named after President Theodore (Teddy) Roosevelt who on a hunting trip in 1902 declined to shoot a black bear that had been chained to a tree.

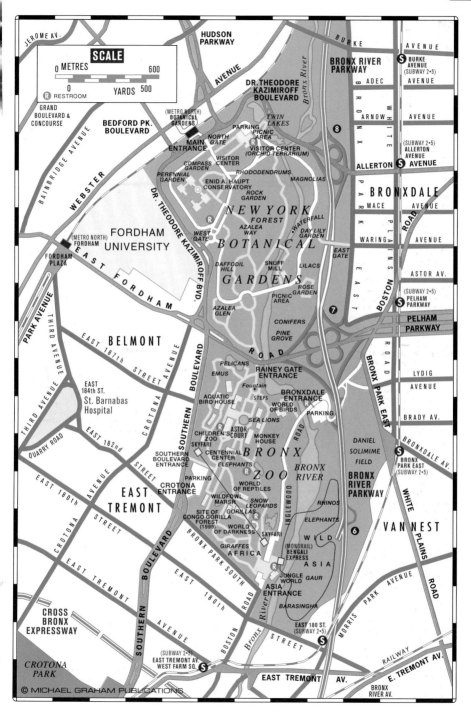

SCALE

0 METRES 600

0 YARDS 500

Ⓡ RESTROOM

JEROME AV.

HUDSON PARKWAY

AVENUE

BURKE

BRONX RIVER PARKWAY

AVENUE

Ⓢ BURKE AVENUE (SUBWAY 2•5)

DR. THEODORE KAZIMIROFF BOULEVARD

ADEC

AVENUE

GRAND BOULEVARD & CONCOURSE

BEDFORD PK. BOULEVARD

(METRO NORTH) BOTANICAL GARDENS

TWIN LAKES

B R O N X

ARNOW

WHITE

AVENUE

PARKING

BAINBRIDGE AVENUE

MAIN ENTRANCE

NORTH GATE

PICNIC AREA

Ⓡ

VISITOR CENTER (ORCHID TERRARIUM)

(SUBWAY 2•5) ALLERTON AVENUE

WEBSTER

COMPASS GARDEN

VISITOR CENTER

RHODODENDRUMS

ALLERTON Ⓢ AVENUE

PERENNIAL GARDEN

ENID A. HAUPT CONSERVATORY

MAGNOLIAS

P A R K

B R O N X D A L E

FORDHAM UNIVERSITY

(METRO NORTH) FORDHAM

Ⓡ

N E W Y O R K FOREST

ROCK GARDEN

MACE

AVENUE

DR. THEODORE KAZIMIROFF BVD.

WEST GATE

AZALEA WAY

•WATERFALL

DAY LILY GARDEN

B O T A N I C A L

WARING

AVENUE

FORDHAM PLAZA

EAST FORDHAM

DAFFODIL HILL

SNUFF MILL

LILACS

EAST GATE

E A S T

ASTOR AV.

PARK AVENUE

G A R D E N S

ROSE GARDEN

BOSTON

PLAINS

(SUBWAY 2•5) PELHAM PARKWAY

THIRD AVENUE

BELMONT

EAST 187th STREET

AZALEA GLEN

PICNIC AREA

CONIFERS

PINE GROVE

7

ROAD

PELHAM PARKWAY

R O A D

LYDIG AVENUE

EAST 184th ST. St. Barnabas Hospital

CROTONA AVENUE

BOULEVARD

PELICANS

EMUS

RAINEY GATE ENTRANCE

Fountain

BRONXDALE ENTRANCE

BRONX PARK EAST

BRADY AV.

THIRD AVENUE

QUARRY ROAD

EAST 182nd STREET

SOUTHERN

AQUATIC BIRD HOUSE

STEPS

WORLD OF BIRDS

PARKING

BRONXDALE AV.

SEA LIONS

Ⓢ BRONX PARK EAST (SUBWAY 2•5)

EAST 180th STREET

EAST TREMONT

Ⓡ

ASTOR COURT

CHILDREN'S ZOO

SKYFARI

MONKEY HOUSE

B R O N X

DANIEL SOLIMIME FIELD

WHITE

SOUTHERN BOULEVARD ENTRANCE

CENTENNIAL CENTER

◇

ELEPHANTS

Z O O

BRONX RIVER

BRONX RIVER PARKWAY

V A N N E S T

PARKING

CROTONA ENTRANCE

WILDFOWL MARSH

Ⓡ

WORLD OF REPTILES

SNOW LEOPARDS

RHINOS

6

EAST TREMONT STREET

SITE OF CONGO GORILLA FOREST (1999)

GORILLAS

WORLD OF DARKNESS

ELEPHANTS

W I L D

CROSS BRONX EXPRESSWAY

BRONX PARK SOUTH

GIRAFFES

A F R I C A

SKYFARI

◇

(MONORAIL) BENGALI EXPRESS

GAUR

A S I A

BRONX RIVER

EAST 180th

BOSTON ROAD

Ⓡ

JUNGLE WORLD

ASIA ENTRANCE

BARASINGHA

MORRIS PARK AVENUE

ROAD

CROTONA PARK

(SUBWAY 2•5) EAST TREMONT AV. WEST FARM SQ.

Ⓢ

EAST 180 ST. (SUBWAY 2•5)

Ⓢ

RAILWAY

EAST TREMONT AV.

E. TREMONT AV.

BRONX RIVER AV.

© MICHAEL GRAHAM PUBLICATIONS

INGLEWOOD ROAD

8

60

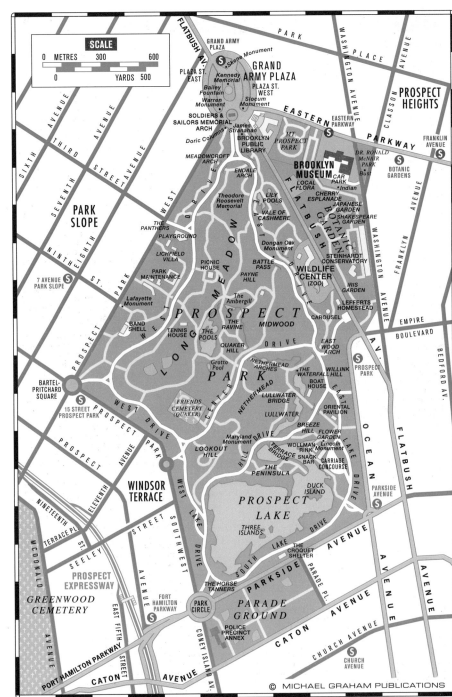

SCALE

| 0 METRES 300 600 |
| 0 YARDS 500 |

FLATBUSH AV.

PARK

GRAND ARMY PLAZA

WASHINGTON AVENUE

PLACE

CLASSON AVENUE

Skene Monument

GRAND ARMY PLAZA

PROSPECT HEIGHTS

PLAZA ST. EAST

Kennedy Memorial

PLAZA ST. WEST

EASTERN

Bailey Fountain

EASTERN PARKWAY

Warren Monument

Slocum Monument

PARKWAY

SOLDIERS & SAILORS MEMORIAL ARCH

FRANKLIN AVENUE

SIXTH AVENUE

THIRD AVENUE

SEVENTH AVENUE

Doric Columns

James Stranahan

MT. PROSPECT PARK

DR. RONALD McNAIR PARK

Bust

MEADOWCROFT ARCH

BROOKLYN PUBLIC LIBRARY

BROOKLYN MUSEUM

CAR PARK

BOTANIC GARDENS

PARK SLOPE

WEST DRIVE

ENDALE ARCH

LOCAL FLORA

Indian

FRANKLYN AVENUE

Theodore Roosevelt Memorial

LILY POOLS

CHERRY ESPLANADE

JAPANESE GARDEN

THE PANTHERS

VALE OF CASHMERE

SHAKESPEARE GARDEN

NINTH ST.

EIGHTH ST.

PLAYGROUND

EAST DRIVE

LICHFIELD VILLA

Dongan Oak Monument

PARK MAINTENANCE

PICNIC HOUSE

BATTLE PASS

STEINHARDT CONSERVATORY

WASHINGTON AVENUE

7 AVENUE PARK SLOPE

PAYNE HILL

WILDLIFE CENTER (ZOO)

PROSPECT PARK WEST

Lafayette Monument

PROSPECT

IRIS GARDEN

EMPIRE

The Ambergill

LEFFERTS HOMESTEAD

BAND SHELL

TENNIS HOUSE

THE POOLS

THE RAVINE

MIDWOOD

CAROUSEL

BOULEVARD

BEDFORD AV.

QUAKER HILL

PARK

DRIVE

EAST WOOD ARCH

PROSPECT PARK

Grotto Pool

NETHERMEAD ARCHES

THE WATERFALL

WILLINK HILL

FRIENDS CEMETERY (QUAKER)

NETHERMEAD

BOAT HOUSE

BARTEL-PRITCHARD SQUARE

WEST

PROSPECT

LULLWATER BRIDGE

LULLWATER

ORIENTAL PAVILION

15 STREET PROSPECT PARK

CENTER

PARK AVENUE

DRIVE

BREEZE HILL

FLOWER GARDEN

Lincoln Monument

PROSPECT

Maryland Monument

WOLLMAN RINK

SNACK BAR

CARRIAGE CONCOURSE

HILL DRIVE

LOOKOUT HILL

TERRACE BRIDGE

EAST LAKE DRIVE

OCEAN

FLATBUSH

WINDSOR TERRACE

THE PENINSULA

DUCK ISLAND

PARKSIDE AVENUE

NINETEENTH ST.

WEST LAKE DRIVE

PROSPECT LAKE

TERRACE PL.

SOUTHWEST AVENUE

THREE ISLANDS

SOUTH LAKE DRIVE

AVENUE

SEELEY ST.

PROSPECT EXPRESSWAY

THE CROQUET SHELTER

PARADE PL.

AVENUE

McDONALD

GREENWOOD CEMETERY

STREET

THE HORSE TANNERS

PARKSIDE

AVENUE

FORT HAMILTON PARKWAY

PARK CIRCLE

PARADE GROUND

CATON

EAST FIFTH STREET

CONEY ISLAND AV.

POLICE PRECINCT ANNEX

AVENUE

CHURCH

PORT HAMILTON PARKWAY

CATON

AVENUE

CHURCH AVENUE

CHURCH AVENUE

© MICHAEL GRAHAM PUBLICATIONS

A DAY IN BROOKLYN

For a day in Brooklyn, you have to be selective, for there is plenty to see. Many people will prefer the walk over the famous bridge and perhaps a leisurely walk along the promenade (Page 48) in the Historic Heights district for the dramatic views of Manhattan, finally turning off down Montague Street (B4 48) for the shops, or Remsen Street (B5 48) for its cafes and restaurants reminiscent of Greenwich Village. It is interesting to note that half the buildings in the Heights district were built before the Civil War; since that time many writers and poets: Auden, Capote, Mailer, Thomas Wolfe, Arthur Miller and Walt Whitman have chosen to live here, and it is understandable why.

PROSPECT PARK
Once again the landscapers of Central Park and Riverside Park - Vaux and Olmsted - combined to design this park which was opened in 1868. They sculpted the terrain and made Prospect Lake and created Grand Army Plaza. The Triumphal Arch came later and was a tribute to the Union forces who died in the Civil War; obvious comparisons are made to the Arc de Triomphe in Paris. The design was by the architect of Grant's Tomb, John H. Duncan. Across from the arch, four eagle-topped Doric columns mark the entrance to the park; here is the place to view the arch which is topped with a striking quadriga - a four-horse bronze chariot. During the summer months the arch is open to the public and it is well worth going to the top for the superb vistas across the park. The park that both architects considered their finest achievement occupies 526 acres. It may have been potentially greater than Central Park, but for me it does not achieve the same heights, nevertheless it still is a remarkable and a very pastoral park for a city.

For information on events and activities in the park, go to the Visitors Center located in the elegant Italianate-style Boathouse which is on Lullwater. Lefferts Homestead, the old Dutch farmhouse, is now a Children's Historic Museum and is open only at weekends from 12.00 to 17.00. Everyone will delight in the sound and color of the Coney Island-style carousel which is situated just outside the zoo entrance.

PROSPECT PARK WILDLIFE CENTER
This little zoo is primarily aimed at children. It is an interactive center with more than 160 animals in natural habitats. Troops of baboons, wallabies, sea lions, an aviary and a Discovery Trail. To go direct take the Subway Line D to Prospect Park.
Daily April - October 10.00 - 17.00. Weekends and holidays 17.30. Nov. - March 10.00 - 16.30 Charge

BROOKLYN BOTANICAL GARDENS
Founded in 1910 on a reclaimed waste tip, this is a beautiful themed garden for all seasons, and it is free! To give you an idea of the variety of plants and garden styles from all over the world that can be seen, there is a Japanese hill and pond garden, a cherry esplanade (lovely in spring), a fragrance garden with 1000 species, and a traditional Elizabethan-style 'knot' herb garden. Inside the conservatory there are orchids, a prize bonsai collection, etc., no need to wear a coat in here! The main entrance is in Washington Avenue and is best approached by Subway line 2 or 3 to Eastern Parkway Station. *Free*
April to Sept. Tues - Fris 8.00 - 18.00. Weekends, holidays 10.00 - 18.00, Oct. to March closes 16.30

BROOKLYN MUSEUM
This is a favorite of mine: a great world-class museum with room to walk around. At the entrance on each side are allegorical female figures representing Manhattan and Brooklyn: originally placed on the Manhattan Bridge - Brooklyn side - and removed after road improvements to their present position in 1963. The building, a six-story structure was built in the Beaux-Arts style and contains diverse exhibits, but is particularly renowned for its Egyptian holdings and for contemporary art - but this is just the tip of an immensely interesting iceberg.

First Floor Free pamphlets will help you in understanding the power sculpture of Africa and the arts of Melanesia where the human form is often represented with animal- and reptile-like figures. There are stone Aztec sculptures from Mexico and a 19th-century North American Blackfoot Indian chief's deerskin tunic.

Second Floor The arts of Asia include beautiful cobalt blue 14c porcelain jars and ceramics: torsos of Buddha from India and Oriental carpets etc.

Third Floor This superb Egyptian collection defines how civilization developed along the Nile. Amongst the decorated sarcophagi (coffins) you will find one of the Sacred Ibis the long-beaked bird - decorated in gold leaf over solid silver and wood, and not far away a 1st century BC alabaster of Alexander the Great: who knows if this is a true resemblance - he died in 323 BC.

Fourth Floor The decorative period rooms range from 1675 to Art Deco 1928 and include the early Dutch farmhouse of Jan Schenk and the smoking room from John D. Rockefeller's brownstone house on West 54th Street. Glass, silver and ceramics are here as well as some interesting fantasy furniture.

Fifth Floor This is probably the floor most people will make for - the European and American art and sculpture. Some highlights are: *Storm in the Rocky Mountains* (1867) a very large and wonderfully atmospheric painting by Albert Bierstadt, the luminous rendering of the *Doges Palace in Venice* (1908) by Claude Monet, *The Shepherdess* (1896), a beautifully textured painting by Daniel Ridgeway Knight. Other artists that might interest you are Georgia O'Keeffe, Degas, Cézanne, Kandinsky, Goya, Pissaro, John Singer Sargent and Winslow Homer. There are also 58 Auguste Rodin bronzes.

Sculpture Garden This small garden is located behind the museum, close by the car park. Pieces saved from the long since demolished Pennsylvania Station and a Lion's Head from the Coney Island amusement park have now found a home here.

Subway Line 2 or 3 will take you close to the museum; the stop is Eastern Parkway. When you come out of the station contemplate that this boulevard was originally intended to emulate the Champs-Élysées in Paris - Grand Army Plaza has the Arch and superb Library....... What happened?
Wednesday to Sunday 10.00 - 17.00   *Charge*

NEW YORK AQUARIUM
Facing the Atlantic off Coney Island boardwalk and established in 1896, the aquarium holds over 10,000 species of fish and marine life in naturalistic settings. Famed for its beluga whales, there are sharks, dolphins, octopi, bright blue lobsters, penguins, etc., inches away! Subway Line F or D to West 8th Street takes you right there.
Daily Monday to Friday 10,00 - 17.00   *Charge*
Summer, weekends and holidays it closes at 19.00

INDEX TO STREETS

ABBREVIATIONS

The letters following a name indicate the Square and Page Number

Al. - Alley	Ct. - Court	Pl. - Place	St. - Street
Av. - Avenue	Dri. - Drive	Plz. - Plaza	Ter. - Terrace
Bd. - Boulevard	E. - East	Prom.- Promenade	Tun.- Tunnel
Bri. - Bridge	La. - Lane	Sth. - South	Wk. - Walk
Cir. - Circle	Nth. - North	Sq. - Square	Wst.- West

MANHATTAN ADDRESS FINDER

APPROXIMATE Delete the last figure of the House Number and divide by 2: then add or subtract the Key Figure eg. to find 500 Park Avenue (Key Figure 34):- 500 divide by 2, add 34 = 59. The answer is between 58th and 60th Streets.

KEY FIGURES

Broadway		5th Avenue		6th Avenue	-12	Columbus Avenue	+60
above 740	-30	*up to 200*	+13	Malcolm X Bd.	+110	10th Avenue	+14
Avenues A·B·C·D	+3	*up to 400*	+16	7th Avenue	+12	Amsterdam Avenue	+60
1st Av. - 2nd Av.	+3	*up to 600*	+18	*above 1780*	+20	11th Avenue	+15
3rd Avenue	+10	*up to 775*	+20	8th Avenue	+10	West End Av.	+60
Lexington Av.	+22	*up to 1282*	-18	Central Park West		Riverside Drive	
Madison Avenue	+26	*up to 1500*	+45	*divide number by 10*	+60	*divide number by 10*	+60
Park Avenue	+34	*up to 2000*	+24	9th Avenue	+13		

East - West numbers divide and begin at 5th Avenue.

Even numbers are usually located on the South Side of the Street.

Traveling North to South - Five Blocks equal very roughly 0 - 100 addresses.

NUMBERED STREETS

East Streets

1st Street C6 40
2-5 Street C5 40
5-9 Street C4 40
10-13 Street B3 40
14-16 Street B2 40
17-20 Street B1 40
21-23 Street C6 36
24-27 Street C5 36
28-30 Street C4 36
31-34 Street C3 36
35-38 Street C2 36
39-41 Street C1 36
42-44 Street C6 32
45-48 Street C5 32
49-52 Street C4 32
53-56 Street C3 32
57-59 Street C2 32
60-63 Street C1 32
64-66 Street D6 28
67-70 Street D5 28
71-73 Street D4 28
74-77 Street C3 28
78-81 Street C2 28
82-84 Street C1 28
85-87 Street C6 24
88-90 Street C5 24
91-94 Street C4 24
95-98 Street C3 24
99-102 Street C2 24
103-105 Street C1 24
106-108 Street H6 21
109-112 Street H5 21
113-116 Street H4 21
117-119 Street H3 21
120-123 Street H2 21
124-127 Street H1 21

West Streets

3-4 Street H5 39
8-9 Street G4 39
10-13 Street F3 39
14-16 Street F2 39
17-20 Street F1 39
21-23 Street G6 35
24-27 Street G5 35
28-30 Street G4 35
31-34 Street G3 35
35-38 Street G2 35
39-41 Street G1 35
42-44 Street E6 31
45-48 Street G5 31
49-52 Street G4 31
53-56 Street G3 31
57-59 Street G2 31
60-63 Street E1 31
64-66 Street E6 26
67-70 Street E5 26
71-73 Street D4 26
74-77 Street D3 26
78-81 Street D2 26
82-84 Street D1 26
85-86 Street D6 22
87-90 Street D5 22
91-94 Street D4 22
95-98 Street D3 22
99-102 Street C2 22
103-105 Street C1 22
106-108 Street C6 22
109-112 Street C5 20
113-116 Street F4 21
117-119 Street F3 21
120-123 Street F2 21
124-127 Street F1 21
128-129 Street D6 19
130-133 Street B5 19
134-137 Street C4 19
138-140 Street B3 19
141-144 Street C2 19
145-148 Street C1 19

A

Abingdon Sq. D3 38
Abraham E. Kazan St. E2 45
Adam Clayton Powell Jr. Boulevard F1 21
Adams Street, Brook. C3 48
Admiral Dewey Prom. C5 46
African Square H1 21
Aitken Pl. Brook. C5 48
Albany Street C2 46
Alexander Hamilton Square C2 19
Allen Street B1 40
Alvin Ailey Pl. D1 30
Amity Street, Brook. C6 48
Amsterdam Av. C1 30-C5 19
Anchorage Pl., Brook. C1 48
Ann Street D1 46
A. Philip Randolph Sq. F3 21
Archbishop Sheen Pl. C6 32
Asser Levy Pl. E5 37
Astor Place A4 40
Atlantic Av., Brook. B6 48
Attorney Street D1 44
Avenue A D4 40
Avenue B E5 41
Avenue C F3 41
Avenue D F4 41
Avenue of the Americas (Sixth Av.) E3 43-G3 31
Avenue of the Finest H6 43

B

Bache Plaza G6 43
Bank Street D4 38
Barclay Street B1 46
Barrow Street E5 39
Baruch Place G6 41
Battery Place B4 46
Baxter Street G3 43
Bayard Street G4 43
Beach Street D4 42
Beaver Street D4 46
Bedford Street E5 39
Beech Street E3 43
Beekman Place E4 33
Beekman Street D1 46
Benson Place F4 43
Bergen Street, Brook. D6 48
Bethune Street D4 38
Bialystoker Pl. D2 44
Bleeker Street G6 39
Bloomfield Street B3 38
Boerum Pl., Brook. D5 48
Bond Street A5 40
Bowery H2 43
Bridge Plz., Brook. D2 48
Bridge Plz.Ct., Brook. D2 48
Bridge Street D4 46
Bridge St., Brook. D1 48
Broad Street D3 46
Broadway D4 46-B2 19
Brooklyn Battery Tun. C3 46
Brooklyn Bridge G1 47
Brooklyn-Queens Expressway, Brook. D1 48
Broome Street G2 43

C

Cadman Plz., Brook. C3 48
Canal Street G3 43
Cannon Street E1 45
Cardinal Hayes Pl. G5 43
Carlisle Street C2 46
Carmine Street F6 39
Cathedral Parkway C5 20
Cathedral Pl., Brook. D3 48
Catherine Lane F4 43
Catherine Slip B5 44
Catherine St. B5 44
Cedar Street D2 46
Central Park Nth. F5 21
Central Pk. Sth. F2 31
Central Pk. Wst.E1 31-E6 21
Centre Market Pl. G2 43
Centre Street G4 43
Chambers Street F5 43
Chapel St., Brook D2 48
Charles Lane D5 38
Chas. Ludlan Corner F4 39
Charles Street D5 38
Charlie Parker Pl. E4 41
Charlton Street D1 42
Chatham Sq. H4 43
Chelsea Sq. D6 34
Cherokee Pl. F2 29
Cherry Street D4 44
Christopher Street E5 39
Chrystie Street A2 44
Church Street F5 43
Claremont Av. B3 20
Clarkson St. E6 39
Clark St., Brook. B3 48
Cleveland Pl. G2 43
Cliff Street E2 47
Clinton Street C1 44
Clinton St., Brook. C4 48
Coenties Al. E4 47
Coenties Slip E4 47
Coleman Sq. C5 44
College Pl., Brook. B4 48
Collister Street D3 42
Cooper Square B4 40
Columbia Hts., Brook. A3 48
Columbia Pl. B5 48
Columbia Street F6 41
Columbia St., Brook. B6 48
Columbus Av. D1 30-D6 20
Commerce Street E5 39
Concord St., Brook. D2 48
Confucius Plaza A4 44
Convent Av. D5 19
Cornelia St. F5 39
Cortlandt Al. F4 43
Cortlandt St. C2 46
Court St., Brook. D5 48
Cranberry St.,Brook. B3 48
Crosby Street G2 43
Cushman Row D6 34

D

Dag Hammarskjold Plaza D5 32
Dean St., Brook. D6 48
Delancey St. A2 44
Delancey St. South E1 45
Depew Place B6 32
Desbrosses St. D3 42
Dey Street C1 46
Diamond and Jewelry Way H5 31
Division Street B4 44
Dominick Street D2 42
Doughty St., Brook. A2 48
Dover Street F1 47
Downing Street F6 39

Doyers Street H4 43
Duane Street E5 43
Duarte Square E3 43
Duffy Square F5 31
Duke Ellington Bd. B6 20
Duke Ellington Cir. H5 21
Dutch Street D1 46
Dvorak Place C1 40
Dyer Avenue D2 34

E
East Broadway B4 44
East End Av. F1 29
East Houston St. C6 41
East Washington
  Street, Brook. B1 48
Edgar Allen Poe St. B1 26
Edgar Street C3 46
Edgecombe Av. D1 19
Eighth Av. D2 38-E3 31
Eldridge Street B1 44
Eleventh Av. B1 38-C5 30
Elizabeth Pl., Brook. A2 48
Elk Street G5 43
Ericsson Pl. E4 43
Esplanade or Promenade,
  Brook. The A4 48
Essex Street C1 44
Evans St., Brook. G5 45
Everitt St., Brook. A2 48
Exchange Alley C3 46
Exchange Pl. D3 46
Extra Pl. B6 40

F
Fann Square E4 43
Fashion Av. F2 35
Father Demo Sq. F5 39
Father Fagan Sq. D1 42
Federal Plaza F5 43
Fifth Avenue G2 39-H1 21
First Avenue C4 40-E2 25
First Place B4 46
Flatbush Avenue ext.
  North Broo. D2 48
Fleet Alley, Brook. B1 48
Fletcher Street E2 47
Foley Square G5 43
Forsyth St. A1 44
Fourth Avenue A3 40
Frank d'Amico Plaza B3 44
Frankfort St. G6 43
Franklin D. Roosevelt
  Drive E4 47-F2 25
Franklin Place F4 43
Franklin Square F1 47
Franklin Street F4 43
Frederick Douglass Bd. E2 21
  Circus E5 21
Freedom Place B5 26
Freeman Alley H1 43
Front Street E3 47-E3 45
Front St., Brook. C1 48
Fulton Street D1 46
Furman Street, Brook. A3 48

G
Gansevoort St. C3 38
Garden Pl., Brook B5 48
Gay Street F4 39
Golda Meir Sq. G1 35
Golden Pacific Plaza C3 43
Gold Street E2 47
Gold St., Brook. G5 45
Gouverneur La. E3 47
Gouverneur Slip E3 45
Gouverneur St. E3 45
Grace Court, Brook. B5 48
Grace Ct. Alley, Brook. B5 48
Gracie Square F6 25
Gracie Terrace F1 29
Gramercy Park C3 34
Grand Army Plaza H2 31
Grand Central Station B6 32
Grand Street A2 44
Great Jones Alley A5 40
Great Jones St. A5 40
Greely Sq. G3 35
Greene St. H6 39
Greenwich Av. E3 39
Greenwich St. D3 36-D4 38
Grove Court E5 39
Grove Street E2 39
Gus d'Amato Way A2 40
Gustave Hartman Sq. E6 31

H
Hamill Place G5 43
Hamilton Pl. C3 19
Hamilton Ter. D2 19

Hancock Place D1 20
Hanover Sq. E3 47
Hanover St. E3 47
Harrison Al., Brook. G6 45
Harrison St. D4 42
Harry Blumenstein Plz. D1 44
Henderson Pl. F6 25
Henry Hudson Parkway
  A4 26-A1 19
Henry J. Browne Bd. D5 22
Henry Street C4 44
Henry St., Brook. B3 48
Herald Square G3 35
Hester St. A3 44
Hicks St., Brook. B3 48
High St., Brook. C2 48
Hogan Pl. G4 43
Holland Tun. Entrance D2 42
Horatio Street C3 38
Howard Al., Brook. B1 48
Howard St. F4 43
Hubert St. D4 42
Hudson Av., Brook. G5 45
Hudson St. E5 43-D3 38
Hunt La., Brook. C5 48

I
Irving Place A2 40

J
Jackson Sq. D3 38
Jackson St. F2 45
James Bogardus
  Triangle E5 43
James Street H5 43
Jay Street D5 42
Jay Street, Brook. D2 48
Jane Street C3 38
Jefferson St. C3 44
Jelly Roll Walk F4 31
Jersey Street G1 43
John de Lury Sr. Plaza E1 47
John H. Finley Walk G6 25
John J. Clavin Pl. G4 43
John J. Lambla Sq. B5 44
Johnson St., Brook. D4 48
John Street E2 47
John St., Brook. F6 45
Jones Alley A6 40
Jones Street F5 39
Joralemon St., Brook. B5 48
Justice John M.
  Harlan Way E4 43

K
Kenmare Street G2 43
Kimlau Square A5 44
King Street D1 42
Korean War Veterans
  Plaza, Brooklyn C3 38

L
Ladies Mile G1 39
Lafayette Court B3 40
Lafayette St. G1 43
La Guardia Place G6 39
Laight St. D3 42
Langston Hughes Pl. H1 21
La Salle Street B1 20
Legion Memorial Sq. E2 27
Lenox Avenue G4 21
Leonard Street F4 43
Leon Davis St. F6 31
Leroy Street D6 38
Lewis Street E1 45
Lexington Av. C5 36-C5 24
Liberty Plaza D2 46
Liberty Street C2 46
Lincoln Center D6 26
Lincoln Square D6 26
Lincoln Tun. Approach D3 34
Lispenard St. E3 43
Little Brazil St. H531
Little Street, Brook. G5 45
Little West 12th St. C3 38
Livingston St., Brook. C5 48
Loisada Av. F4 41
Louise Nevelson Plaza E2 47
Love Lane, Brook. B4 48
Ludlow Street B1 44

M
MacDougal Alley G4 39
MacDougal St. G6 39
Madison Av. B4 36-H3 21
Madison Square A5 36
Madison Street C4 44
Maiden Lane D2 46
Main St., Roosevelt I. G4 29

Main Street, Brook. B1 48
Malcom X Boulevard G2 21
Mangin St. G641
Manhattan Al. F5 43
Manhattan Av. E1 23-D3 20
Manhattan Bridge B2 20
Marginal Street E4 45
Marketfield St. D4 46
Market Slip C5 44
Market Street B4 44
Marshall St., Brook. G5 45
Martin Luther King Jr.
  Boulevard E1 21
McCarthy Square E4 39
Mercer Street H6 39
Middagh St., Brook. B2 48
Miller Highway B1 30-B6 26
Milligan Pl. F3 39
Mill Lane E3 47
Minetta Lane F5 39
Minetta St. F5 39
Mitchell Place E4 33
Monroe Place C4 48
Monroe St. B5 44
Montague St., Brook. B4 48
Montague Ter., Brook. B5 48
Montefiore Sq. B3 19
Montgomery St. D4 44
Moore Street D4 46
Morningside Av. D2 20
Morningside Dri. D3 20
Morris St. C3 46
Morton St. E6 39
Mosco Street H4 43
Mt. Morris Park West G2 21
Mulberry St. G2 43
Mulry Square E3 39
Murray St. E6 43

N
Nassau Street D1 46
Nassau St., Brook. D2 48
Nathan D. Perlman Pl. C2 40
Navy Street, Brook. H6 45
New Dock St., Brook. A1 48
New Street D3 46
Ninth Avenue C2 38-D5 30
Norfolk Street C1 44
North End Av. A1 46
North Moore St. D4 42

O
Old Broadway C5 19
Old Fulton St., Brook. A2 48
Old Slip E3 47
Oliver St. A5 44
Orange St., Brook. B3 48
Orchard St. B1 44

P
Pace Plaza G6 43
Pacific St., Brook. C6 48
Park Avenue B3 36-B3 24
Park Avenue South B6 36
Park Place E6 43
Park Pl. West C6 42
Park Row H5 43
Park Street D5 46
Patchin Pl. F3 39
Pearl St. D4 47-G5 43
Pearl St., Brook. B5 48
Peck Slip F1 47
Pell Street H4 43
Penn Plaza F3 35
Peretz Square D6 40
Perry Street D4 38
Peter Cooper Rd. E6 37
Peter Minuit Plaza D5 46
Pierrepont Pl., Brook. B4 48
Pierrepont St., Brook. B4 48
Pierre Toussaint Sq. C1 42
Pike Street C4 44
Pineapple St., Brook. B4 48
Pine Street C3 46
Pitt Street D1 44
Platt Street E2 47
Plymouth St., Brook. F6 45
Police Plaza G5 43
Pomander Walk C4 42
Poplar St., Brook. B2 48
Prince St. E1 43
Printing House Sq. G6 43
Prospect St., Brook. C2 48

Q
Queensboro Bridge F2 33
Queensboro Bri. Plaza D1 32
Queens Midtown Tunnel
  Approach Rd. E2 37

R
Reade Street F5 43
Rector Place B3 46
Rector Street C3 46
Red Cross Pl., Brook. C2 48
Reinhold Niebuhr Pl. B2 20
Remsen Street, Brook. B5 48
Renwick St. C2 42
Republican Al. F5 43
Restaurant Row E5 31
Rheda Liebowitz Sq. E2 45
Ridge Street D1 44
River Road G4 29
Riverside Drive B3 26-B4 19
Riverside Drive
  East and West A1 20
Riverside Dri. Viaduct. A6 19
River Terrace C6 42
River View Ter. F2 33
Rivington St. C1 44
Robert F. Wagner Sr.
  Place A6 44
Rockefeller Center H4 31
Rockefeller Plaza H4 31
Roosevelt Island Bri. H4 39
Roosevelt Sq. D1 20
Rutgers Slip D4 44
Rutgers St. C4 44
Rutherford Pl. B2 20
Ryders Alley E1 47

S
St. Clair Place B6 19
St. James Pl. H6 43
St. John's La. E3 43
St. Luke's Pl. E6 39
St. Mark's Pl. C2 40
St. Nicholas Av. E3 21-D1 19
St. Nicholas Ter. D5 19
St. Vincent's Sq. E3 39
Samuel A. Spiegel Sq. F2 45
Samuel Dickstein Plz. D2 44
Samuel Marx Triangle F4 21
Sand St., Brook. C2 48
Schermerhorn Row F2 47
Schermerhorn Street
  Brooklyn C5 48
Second Avenue C4 40-D4 24
Second Pl. B4 46
Seventh Avenue E1 39-F4 31
Seventh Av. Sth. F4 39
Sheridan Sq. F4 39
Sherman Sq. D4 26
Shinbone Al. A5 40
Shona Bailey Pl. B4 19
Sixth Avenue E3 43-G3 31
  (Av. of the Americas)
Sniffen Court C2 46
South End Av. B3 46
South Street E4 47-D4 44
South St. Seaport G2 47
South William St. D4 46
Spring St. G2 43
Spruce St. G6 43
Stable Court B5 40
Stable Street E5 43
Stanton Street C6 41
State St. D4 46
State St., Brook. B6 48
Stone Street E4 47
Stonewall Place F4 39
Straus Square C3 44
Stuyvesant Sq. C2 40
Stuyvesant St. B4 40
Suffolk St. C1 44
Sullivan St. G6 39
Sutton Place E2 33
Sutton Pl. South E3 33
Sutton Sq. F2 33
Swing St. G4 31
Sidney Place, Brook. C5 48
Szold Place F3 41

T
Taras Chevchenko Pl. B4 40
Technical Pl., Brook. D1 48
Tenth Avenue B1 38-C5 30
Thames Street C2 46
Theater Row D6 30
Theatre Alley F4 43
Thelonius Monk Circle C6 26
Third Avenue B3 40-C5 24
Third Place B3 46
Thomas Street E5 43
Thompson Street E2 43
Tiemann Place B6 19
Tillary St., Brook. D3 48
Times Square F6 31
Tompkins Square D4 40
Triborough Bridge H1 25
Trimble Place F5 43
Trinity Place C2 46

64

Cover and Page 1 Illustrations
by Ronald Maddox PRI, FCSD.

First Published 1998
1 2 3 4 5 6 7 8 9 10

My thanks to Kristine Puopolo who helped me prepare the
text and devised the walks, and of course my wife Joan
who trudged the streets of Manhattan with me.

PENGUIN BOOKS

Published by the Penguin Group
Penguin Books Ltd, Wrights Lane, London W8 5TZ, England
Penguin Putnam Inc., 375 Hudson Street, New York, New York 10014, USA
Penguin Books Australia Ltd., Ringwood, Victoria, Australia
Penguin Books Canada Ltd., 10 Alcorn Avenue, Toronto, Ontario, Canada M4V 3B2
Penguin Books (NZ) Ltd, 182-190 Wairau Road, Auckland 10, New Zealand
Penguin Books Ltd., Registered Offices: Harmondsworth, Middlesex, England